## Also by Phillip D. Reisner

Whispering
Time Remnants
Letters to Angela
I See Movies In My Head
Dichotomy
Forgive Me When I Falter

# Two Days in Superior Court One

Phillip D. Reisner

Order this book online at www.trafford.com
or email orders@trafford.com

Most Trafford titles are also available at major online book retailers.

Print information available on the last page.

ISBN: 978-1-4907-7273-8 (sc)
ISBN: 978-1-4907-7275-2 (hc)
ISBN: 978-1-4907-7274-5 (e)

Library of Congress Control Number: 2016906587

*Trafford rev. 04/22/2016*

 www.trafford.com

North America & international
toll-free: 1 888 232 4444 (USA & Canada)
fax: 812 355 4082

# *Preface*

I studied the Constitution during the past couple of years, finding it a wonderful, unique document that is beautiful and enduring. The more I delved into early American history the more I realized what a work of art both the Constitution and the Declaration of Independence were when written and continue to be today. I always admired Thomas Jefferson and knew a little bit about Aristotle and John Locke, but I gained a better understanding of how our Republic was formed and to where we as a free people should be heading by studying the Constitution.

I included some information about Thomas Jefferson and much about several aspects of our country in this book. I combined my experience of serving on a jury through narrative while reflecting my privately held feelings about our Republic and the general concept of freedom through poetic expression.

I practiced the philosophy of "Know Thyself" since my senior year in high school. It has been a silent mantra and an applied idea during most of my life. I remember when my first prospective employer asked about my favorite book and I replied, "Plato's Republic." It probably sounded a little strange at that time at the age of eighteen, but it was true and meaningful to me then and yet today. I never abandoned the reasoning of self-evaluation, acceptance of who I naturally am and the willingness to adapt to a given environment. I concentrated on learning about myself and teaching others to do the same for a long time. The thing I remembered most about the book Plato's Republic was "Know Thyself." Oh, I knew a little bit about Socrates, Plato and Aristotle; but I didn't realize that they were all teachers and also indirectly co-founders of our Republic long before it was even a gleam in the eyes of a few revolutionary American Founders.

I have always appreciated philosophy and developed some feeble philosophy of my own. I try to convey it through my books. I hope this book puts a personal perspective on freedom, exposes my views concerning our Republic and conveys how the jury system fits into the whole beautiful American experiment. I began to appreciate and better understand the process of serving on a jury when finally getting the chance to fulfill a long desired wish.

The Bill of Rights is actually the first ten amendments to the Constitution of the United States. Amendment VI of the Bill of Rights states that a person accused of any criminal crime shall have the right to a speedy and public trial by an impartial jury. The State of Indiana has different types of juries. It is a state that requires twelve selected peers to judge a person's guilt or innocence of any accused criminal crime.

o

# *Bill of Rights*

### *Amendment I*
*Congress shall make no law respecting an establishment of religion, or prohibiting the free exercise thereof; or abridging the freedom of speech, or of the press; or the right of the people peaceably to assemble, and to petition the Government for a redress of grievances.*

### *Amendment II*
*A well regulated Militia, being necessary to the security of a free State, the right of the people to keep and bear Arms, shall not be infringed.*

### *Amendment III*
*No Soldier shall, in time of peace be quartered in any house, without the consent of the Owner, nor in time of war, but in a manner to be prescribed by law.*

### *Amendment IV*
*The right of the people to be secure in their persons, houses, papers, and effects, against unreasonable searches and seizures, shall not be violated, and no Warrants shall issue, but upon probable cause, supported by Oath or affirmation, and particularly describing the place to be searched, and the persons or things to be seized.*

### *Amendment V*
*No person shall be held to answer for a capital, or otherwise infamous crime, unless on a presentment or indictment of a Grand Jury, except in*

*cases arising in the land or naval forces, or in the Militia, when in actual service in time of War or public danger; nor shall any person be subject for the same offence to be twice put in jeopardy of life or limb; nor shall be compelled in any criminal case to be a witness against himself, nor be deprived of life, liberty, or property, without due process of law; nor shall private property be taken for public use, without just compensation.*

### Amendment VI
*In all criminal prosecutions, the accused shall enjoy the right to a speedy and public trial, by an impartial jury of the State and district wherein the crime shall have been committed, which district shall have been previously ascertained by law, and to be informed of the nature and cause of the accusation; to be confronted with the witnesses against him; to have compulsory process for obtaining witnesses in his favor, and to have the Assistance of Counsel for his defense.*

### Amendment VII
*In Suits at common law, where the value in controversy shall exceed twenty dollars, the right of trial by jury shall be preserved, and no fact tried by a jury, shall be otherwise re-examined in any Court of the United States, than according to the rules of the common law.*

### Amendment VIII
*Excessive bail shall not be required, nor excessive fines imposed, nor cruel and unusual punishments inflicted.*

### Amendment IX
*The enumeration in the Constitution, of certain rights, shall not be construed to deny or disparage others retained by the people.*

### Amendment X
*The powers not delegated to the United States by the Constitution, nor prohibited by it to the States, are reserved to the States respectively, or to the people.*

o

A judge in an Indiana court has the responsibility of setting the punishment of a person if found guilty by a jury. That appears to relieve the jury of punishment responsibility, but that is only partially true because finding a person guilty puts the guilty person in the hands of the judge to decide punishment according to the guidelines of the law. I think the judge has several discretionary considerations, but the juror yet has partial responsibility. That is why from the beginning of my jury experience, I realized that a person's life was partially in my hands. I could not just hand off all responsibility to a judge, wipe my hands clean and not be held partially accountable for the verdict and thus the outcome of the verdict.

Amendment VI reveals that a trial shall take place in the state or district where the crime was committed. Our case was in Tippecanoe County and particularly, in Lafayette, Indiana. The trial on which I was asked to jury serve took place in the beautiful Tippecanoe County Courthouse.

I had never entered the courthouse before the morning of May 20, 2014. I lived in Tippecanoe County for eight years, walked around the courthouse many times, but never took a tour or been required to enter.

Amendment VI also states that a person must be informed about the nature and cause of the crime that he or she is accused. The prosecution and the defense can, by means of the court and lawyers, provide witnesses for and against the accused.

I was very ignorant of the law, courts and the jury system. I remained quite ignorant of the law and its execution even after learning much in a short period of time while studying the Constitution. I waited a long time to be educated about the jury system. I looked forward to being selected, but thought the odds were against me because there were many people from whom to choose. I remained hopeful, but wary about the possibility of jury duty selection.

I had no idea about what the case would concern. I had previously been asked to serve in a petit jury pool. The prospective trial didn't take place and I was not needed. It was settled out of court. I had no knowledge or experience advantage over anyone else called to serve. It seems most people know about the law, courtrooms and trials mainly from that viewed on TV. I was as ignorant as the next person, and to be honest, I remained pretty ignorant about the law even after serving. It is complicated.

I guessed that most people would rather not get too close to a courtroom unless required. I personally appeared before a judge once when sixteen for having a loud exhaust on my car. I got several speeding tickets when I was under twenty-one and had to go before a Justice of the Peace a couple of times. A judge took my driver's license away for three months when I was twenty-one. I reluctantly participated in two courtroom hearings in my forties when dealing with divorce and child visitation. I yet consider myself as having little contact with the judicial system.

I visited a courtroom a long time ago to watch a lawyer friend of mine defend a young woman who was accused of killing an old lady with a brick. She, of course, was deemed innocent in accordance with the law. Jim did his best to provide her with a fair trial, but in the end she was found guilty by the jury. The outcome was no surprise to anyone.

My friend was meticulous about every word, statement and question. To be honest it was quite boring and I didn't last but a few days observing. I was sure Jim did a marvelous job representing her while it being nearly impossible to defend her. It was a long drawn out process. I heard that most trials last only a couple of days. I was surprised to hear that statistic because of the long trials covered by the media on TV. I guess short trials aren't exciting enough for the general public to watch and hear about on the news.

I never had any serious experiences with the law, even though I was on the wrong side of the law a few times in my younger years. I tended to drive too fast in my fifty-seven customized Chevy. I also ditched the cops successfully three times without realizing the seriousness at the time. I later realized it was actually a serious crime with serious consequences. I was very young, stupid and lucky. Everyone needs a little luck now and then. I have been lucky my whole life, not having to suffer but a few consequences for my stupidity.

I never liked being in a position to judge others, yet serving on a jury is being willing to judge one's peers. My situation was a dichotomy and I was caught in the middle of it. I didn't want to judge others while at the same time wanted to put myself in a position to judge others. The whole process of jury duty appeared to be a definite dichotomy unless a juror has strong feelings one way or another.

I considered writing about my experience as a juror from the moment I entered the courthouse. I, however, didn't think it would affect me very much; after all I am seventy-three years old and have had a lot of life changing experiences. I was wrong.

My father lectured me on complicated subjects like responsibility, decision making and consequences a long time ago. He broke it down into simple terms and clear examples. He was a man of few words, but they were direct and powerful words. He was a philosopher with no formal education.

I developed my own philosophy over many years while concerning self and societal behavior, and attempted to share it with my children for forty years and with middle and high school students for thirty years.

I began collecting thoughts about the emotional and enlightening experience of serving on a jury; starting out by writing only a few words about the experience. I had no idea it would affect me like it finally did, compelling me to record the process while renewing my passion for freedom. I started writing poems about the founding of our Republic, Declaration of Independence, Constitution and Bill of Rights quite some time ago, not realizing I would someday use them in a book about the jury system. I discovered that freedom is the glue holding both individual liberty and societal jury duty together.

Some people in the original group of 37 selected for jury duty wished not to serve. I, however, was eager to serve. Some people tried to dodge serving while others didn't believe they qualified to serve for one reason or another. I was ready, willing and able to serve. Someone one said the law requires everyone to serve if selected to serve; only a truly critical excuse is acceptable for one to not serve. I was prepared to serve before I even got there at that time and place in the Tippecanoe County courthouse on May 20, 2014.

# Contents

**Chapter IV - Courtroom** ............................................. 117

# Introduction

I had lived in several places, owned property, paid taxes and voted yet never was selected for jury duty. I had watched jury trials on TV, fictional and real, and wished to be part of the process. It was odd how others around me were called for jury duty, but I never heard a word.

I thought about the jury system and decided my chances of getting selected were slim, considering that I lived most of my life in Montgomery County with a population of over 38,000 and Tippecanoe County with a population of over 177,000. I was surely an insignificant person, sort of a sand grain in the desert of humanity.

I filled out a questionnaire sent to me the previous year concerning jury duty in Tippecanoe County. That was a good start towards being selected, then was summoned to the court house about six months later. I phoned the courthouse number as instructed to see if I was needed for the jury pool and discovered the trial would not take place. I was not needed.

My mind worked overtime thinking about the next invitation to serve. My imagination formulated possibilities while thinking at light speed, but there was little information and understanding about the jury system on which to ponder. I could only fantasize. I paid attention to how I might fit into the whole natural organic system of life while thinking about our man made system of government, the jury system in particular. The whole idea of serving on a jury sparked learning about living in a free Republic. I studied on line about the Constitution through a course call Constitution 101 provided by Hillsdale College. I even visited the Hillsdale campus during one summer and took many pictures. I put a few of those pictures in the book. It is an impressive place, but what they do to further knowledge of our form of government is even more impressive. I suggest everyone take the course. They ask for a fifty dollar donation, but it's not necessary. I donated fifty dollars to Hillsdale College several times so that others might take the course at no cost.

*Phillip D. Reisner*

My free American mind continued to think, speak and write about rights and responsibilities for all. I wrote about my personal interpretation of life, liberty and the pursuit of happiness.

I remembered ideas learned in school, on TV and during elections. I learned basic governmental philosophy while taking the Constitution 101 course. The whole freedom thing began to make sense as I studied the Declaration of Independence, Constitution and Bill of Rights. I learned that our Republic stands alone in the world as a beacon of hope and an outline for success. I began anticipating the reality of practicing my fundamental rights of life, liberty and the pursuit of happiness. I began to anticipate writing this book and sharing my experience of serving on a criminal trial jury.

I wrote this book of narratives and poems for you, your consideration and your help in preserving our wonderful Republic. It seems like we are presently engaged in an important government and society change. It also seems like many aspects of our way of life are being turned upside down. The whole world seems like a scary place to presently live. It's almost like the world is on the brink of revolution in one form or another. I hope this book puts a bit of reality into how the United States of America was founded and why we "The People" must return to constitutional fundamentals.

# Chapter I

# *Waiting To Serve*

# May 20, 2014 - 7:15

I got a letter on May 12, 2014 requesting my presence at the county courthouse to possibly serve on a jury in Tippecanoe County Superior Court 1. My request letter gave a phone number to call to learn if the trial would take place. I was excited and couldn't wait to make the call. The clock moved slowly while I waited until after 4:30 pm to call and get final instructions for appearing or not at the courthouse. I called and heard that indeed the trial was scheduled. I was told through the phone message when and where to appear. I didn't sleep very well that night before appearing and got up early. I ate breakfast, showered and sat waiting for the slow moving clock to display 7:15 am. It finally clicked to the 7:15 mark, my calculated time to leave the house. I crawled into my Cherokee Jeep and headed for the Tippecanoe County Courthouse located in downtown Lafayette, Indiana.

The legal questionnaire received in 2013 required answers to questions about many aspects of my life so that someone at a later date might have a profile of experience, education, beliefs and character. It apparently provided the chance for me to finally serve on a jury.

I anxiously drove towards the designated jury parking lot. I remembered passing the lot when cutting through from 2nd Street to head south on 3rd Street. It used to be covered with white rock and had a small sign that was difficult to read. I wasn't sure its use in the past. It, however, had been newly paved and had a large brightly painted sign that read "Jury Parking Only."

It had clean white parking space stripes. Most of the spaces were already taken by the time I arrived. I was worried about being late, but was reassured after checking my Jeep clock. I leisurely walked towards the courthouse which was three blocks away.

A few other people were walking in my direction; some coming from the jury parking lot, probably heading for the same place as me. Several of us lined up near the two modern metal courthouse doors that contrasted greatly with the old courthouse stone and concrete surrounding them. They opened to a physical inspection point operated by a Tippecanoe County deputy sheriff who stopped and checked everyone entering the courthouse.

I stood for a several minutes outside the courthouse waiting with other people until 7:45 am, the time allowed to enter the courthouse.

I had plenty of time to think about the Forefathers who prophetically wrote about my presence here in the courthouse long ago. I never realized their brilliance until studying the Declaration of Independence and the Constitution. They knew I would someday be in this place, doing this thing. The Declaration of Independence reads as follows.

*"When in the Course of human events, it becomes necessary for one people to dissolve the political bands which have connected them with another, and to assume among the powers of the earth, the separate and equal station to which the Laws of Nature and of Nature's God entitle them a decent respect to the opinions of mankind requires that they should declare the causes of which impel them to the separation."*

It continues to read:

> *"We hold these truths to be self-evident, that all men are created equal, that they are endowed by their Creator with certain unalienable Rights that among these are Life, Liberty and the pursuit of Happiness--"*

Fifty-six courageous men who signed the Declaration of Independence were from Georgia, North Carolina, South Carolina, Massachusetts, Pennsylvania, Maryland, Virginia, Delaware, New York, New Jersey, New Hampshire, Rhode Island and Connecticut. Jefferson wrote the minds and hearts of the American people. The political philosophy was certainly not new. It went back in time to Aristotle and John Locke, but Jefferson summarized the "self-evident truths" or the real grievances against the King of England. I sort of felt like Jefferson was standing in line with me there at the courthouse entry to be security cleared.

The Founders predicted and insured their wisdom through divine guidance. I sensed their presence, nearly heard their words and faintly saw parts the Constitution in my mind as I waited to help execute justice.

I remembered a person is presumed innocent and must be found guilty beyond a reasonable doubt. The idea of deciding someone's guilt or innocence weighed heavy on my mind because another's life might soon be in my hands; another's freedom might be at stake if I was chosen for jury duty. I was there in that place because freedom is the foundation of our American way of life. I thanked the Lord for living in the United States of America.

I reflected about being at home, recalling those glorious words "We the People" while looking at the American flag situated outside my living room window.

    I habitually sat in my big Lazy Boy chair, it was my office; from there I watched TV, listened to music, emailed and wrote. That was where a free American mind consistently got expressed by way of a marvelous writing computing tool. I routinely thanked God there in that Lazy Boy chair for my precious eyes, hands and brain that allowed me to write.

    My mind jerked back to reality when someone loudly said, "Next." I took everything out of my pockets and removed my belt for scanning before passing through the magnetometer.

Some people had to remove their shoes. I passed through security without a problem, and quickly re-looped my belt after collecting wallet and keys.

I headed towards the second floor by way of steps to my left after the security check. There was an elevator available, but I preferred the steps, suspecting the need for exercise due to probably sitting during much of the day. I had no idea how a jury was selected, but knew there were many people who went through security, most of whom were surely there for jury selection. I passed four sculpted replicas of noted people in Tippecanoe County history like John Purdue and Tecumseh.

Tecumseh was a Native American leader of the Shawnee Indians and an influential person in Tippecanoe County. He settled in Prophetstown, just north of Lafayette. I couldn't help but think about his impact on the community when I saw him immortalized in stone there in the courthouse. His face showed resolve. I had resolve.

I walked onward through a wide hall decorated with stone, wood and plaster. The original metal elevator moved up and down to my left. It was hard to believe the building was over a hundred and thirty years old. It took three years to construct it with evident skill and precision. It yet looked nearly new. I was impressed with the building, how well it had been maintained and complemented with paintings and sculptures.

I cleared the first set of stairs made of granite slabs complemented by pinkish granite stairwell walls. There was a wide second floor expanse at the top of the stairs that displayed more paintings. I stopped to look at the artist's name on one of the paintings; it was painted by the same person as a painting at home.

No wonder I liked it. I liked the artist's work a couple years earlier. at the Art Around the Fountain art show held every summer on the courthouse square.

Looking further into history caused me to think more about the Constitution. Everything around me gave a better understanding of my inherited life, liberty and pursuit of happiness. Freedom surely seeps into one's soul.

Our founders didn't gain a republican philosophy easily or overnight. It was in the making for a couple thousand years. Our Forefathers didn't come up with the idea that a natural human being could rule himself or herself on their own. The idea was not new, but the act of making it possible was innovative. Thank God for the United States of American and all those who have made it possible. It is up to us to keep the philosophy going.

We are obliged to exercise our freedom. Too bad people aren't required to be well informed and vote, but then I guess we have the freedom to vote or not vote. We deserve who we vote or don't vote into office. Our continuation of freedom is based on a limited number of people voting because the majority of citizens don't vote. It's a real shame more people don't vote.

Well, forty-seven people had been summoned to potentially serve on a jury. I heard somewhere that one has to vote in order to be selected to serve on a jury. I didn't know if that was true.

I continued to observe the beautiful courthouse with its Neoclassic Architecture. More paintings hung on every hallway representing several local and regional artists. I took a left turn on the third floor where Superior Court One was located and recognized another person's painting I had at home. I apparently have good taste in art.

I continued to be inspired by the courthouse; beginning to imagine what the courtroom would look like. My mind gathered historical symbolism and potential.

I reasoned the courtroom would follow the same theme of oak carved wood as in the grand courthouse halls and doors. Engrossing history moved from one observation place to another and to one floor to another. Even the hinges on the huge oak doors were forged decorative iron. They had to be sturdy in order to hold the heavy weight of thick oak doors for a hundred and thirty years and beyond.

I perpetuated history by acknowledging existence of the place, and if chosen to serve on a jury, I would make history by participating in the judicial process conducted in the building. I felt blessed with aware eyes and mind. I paused to look upward through two levels of courthouse rotunda to see a decorative glass dome that allowed sunlight to filter through to the first floor.

Some people were waiting for hearings and some for trials. No one smiled or joked; it was a serious place. I was serious myself, thinking about what might happen and guessing about how it might happen.

I had plenty of time to get to where I belonged. I had given myself time to drive to downtown, walk to the courthouse, pass through a metal detector and climb two sets of stairs. I left phone and thus clock in the Jeep; my internal clock said I had plenty of time.

I walked through and into a different world, a world of architectural design and construction not applied today. Every county in the State of Indiana had a beautiful courthouse built at the county seat. I pleasantly thought about those courthouses, wishing a picture of each.

I continued to stroll left, finally being directed by a sign that read "Jury Duty." Another similar sign pointed towards a room outfitted with a large table surrounded by chairs. Other chairs were placed on the room's perimeter. Several people were there waiting for further instructions.

I couldn't help but think about ugliness, sorrow and guilt, and about beauty, joy and innocence that had occupied this wonderful place since 1884. A lot of work went into courthouse construction;. a lot of work got accomplished during its many years of prominent existence.

People kept arriving, taking a seat and speaking little; they all seemed to be in a zone while waiting for further instructions. I guessed most didn't know what was about to happen. Thirteen people didn't show and there were forty-seven of us who did follow the summons to appear. Those thirteen people were surely in trouble. The law requires people to appear for jury duty and serve the community if summoned.

We waited for nearly an hour. The bailiff finally arrived and introduced herself, collected names and jury appointed numbers. I was tentatively summoned as jury number 191. She finished explaining what was about to happen, then called out the first thirteen people who would enter the jury box for questioning by the prosecuting and defense attorneys.

I was temporarily declared as juror number five, taking that as a good sign of being selected; thinking early selection was probably based on the previously mailed survey. I guessed someone thought I was a good choice for the jury. We lined up in a row of thirteen, one person being the alternate, and waited for the bailiff to say "All rise."

We walked single file into the courtroom, past two tables designated for prosecution and defense lawyers, and the defendant. We finally stepped into the jury box and continued to stand until the judge said "You may be seated."

I anxiously sat in a place thought about for a very long time. I was in that seat seen on TV, read about in the newspapers and dreamed about at night. I was in a new place of responsibility. I was not in school learning, Navy spying or classroom teaching; I was where Thomas Jefferson and the Founders had constitutionally designed. It was where lives got changed, ruined or reprieved; where a person might remain free or have liberties dismantled.

I was in a place of deeply held respect, where all stood when I entered and where my final opinion was very important. I was an unimportant person made important by sheer presence. It required all to do something important, made important by Thomas Jefferson a long time ago.

I was born unimportant to the world in Terre Haute, Indiana and lived there for twenty-three years until going to Bremerhaven, Germany to serve in the Navy for two years. I lived and taught school in Crawfordsville, Indiana for thirty years until meeting Deborah Bennett, then moved to Lafayette, Indiana. I was a Hoosier for sure, pretending to be a Floridian on two occasions, but it never stuck.

Debi and I had vacationed in Florida during the winter for a few months for several years, but that didn't make me a Floridian. There wasn't a Florida license plate on my truck to match the Florida boat plate. I continued as a lifer in Indiana and expected to die in Indiana. I felt very Hoosier-like sitting in the jury box with fellow Hoosiers. The Indiana seal seen earlier on the third floor depicting an 1816 environment kept flashing through my mind while Thomas Jefferson's ghost whispered to my Hoosier soul.

# Unique Idea

Upon a
foundation,
I shall
build a
house of
integrity and
beauty,
where I shall
live freely and
find security.
Block by block,
wall by wall,
shingle by shingle,
I shall
work
my hands and
mind until
task is completed.
Warm sun
shall penetrate
my windows,
gentle rain
shall caress
my roof, and
I shall
rejoice with
my brothers.
And to think,
it all
began with an
idea in
my unique
mind.

# Sought Truth

Through
ship portholes
men witnessed
wisdom and
gained meaning as
insight fostered
natural truth
while sailing an
alien ocean.

Hope resided
within past,
present and
scary future, and
composed
everything anew,
intoxicated
necessity and
blinded restraint.

Pilgrims sought
tomorrow as if
already knowing
truth today,
found born
again reality
thriving,
thus tended
to tomorrow.

Time weighed
even less than
thought and
both moved at
light speed,

ideas changed,
got renewed and
sought
natural minds.

And through
purely discovered
mind windows,
placed and
glazed with insight,
they perceived
freedom clearly
by thought and
reasoning.

Forefathers got
new meaning,
awareness and
natural truth
through mind
portholes that
pilgrims planted
three hundred
years earlier.

# Predestined

We gathered
often and long,
discussing what
kind of wall
to build, and
from deliberations
came ideas that
seemed predestined,
for we agreed on
nearly everything.
Certain truths
were evident.
Beauty arose and
all were pleased at
construction's end.
Our plan served
intentions and
requirements.
We felt secure
within our
raised walls of
will and design.
A collection of
new ideas
brought hope and
faith to an
effective system.
Consensus meant
obligation and
obligation meant
responsibility.
We were united.

# Natural Earth

Sun is gracious to sky,
sky respects soil and
all that grows overtly
flourishes in civility.
Of course,
there are days
when rain punishes
soil and sun,
bakes everything
too much, but
in final analysis,
everything finds
politeness with a
few scars and
evidential changes.

Sun makes everything
happen and so it is
no wonder that light
wins over darkness and
good defeats evil.
Earth wishes to
be civilized.
Man learns from
natural Earth.
Natural rights and
responsibilities are
Higher Power shared,
teaching moments
occurring every day and
every night.

# Springtime

Springtime
flowers gather
attention every
day with purples,
violets, reds,
whites and oranges.
It's like a
collection of ideas
based on some
common goal that
gives a hopeful
continuum of
colorful days.
It's no
different from
Jefferson and
Adams long ago,
bringing ideas and
allowing them to
red, white and
blue blossom.
A few men beget
ideas greater than
most imagined.
New national
spring was a
glorious time for
more than
assorted gazing.
It was a time for
full attention and
bold planting.

# Reflections

Who has not felt a
firm clasping hand,
mind meeting mind,
destiny affirming?

Nature silently grows
wanton ideas that
flourish like sun
brightly glistening
off churning water,
while noisily reflecting
its agitated desire for
evolving freedom to
establish a nation.

Who has not felt a
firm clasping hand,
mind meeting mind,
destiny affirming?

In silent minds
where ideas spawn,
comes bright faith,
but like tattered sails
noisily flapping in
willing ocean wind,
natural human spirits
conquer wilderness
and grow freedom.

# A Statue

A block of
untainted granite,
God created,
Earth formed and
Man chiseled,
became more
by becoming less.

Artists sculpted
silent stone into a
speaking statue to
long persevere
while creating a
heroic figure to
Republic signify.

Granite, "Faith,"
points heavenly with
bible in hand to
remind Pilgrims and
colonists to extol
Freedom, Morality,
Law and Education.

Graceful beauty
seeks hearts, minds
and souls on a
Plymouth street,
1820 conceived and
1889 dedicated as
Lady Faith.

# Aristotle's Art

Can time affect
art well,
collect brilliant
ideas through
nature while
radiant moments
centuries pause?

Can anyone
imagine a thing
created on
principles or
philosophize a
future sun in
heavenly sky?

Can a people
provide beauty in
living days on
earth's rich shell,
pleasing eyes,
changing moods,
causing freedom?

Can a document
speak louder
than words, and
form a more
perfect union of
humanity and
art?

Can Aristotle's
artful dialectic
yet liberate and
design a national
philosophy as if
thousands of years
never passed?

I ask again can
time affect art well,
collect brilliant
ideas through
nature while
radiant moments
centuries pause?

My answer
lies with Socrates,
Plato and
Aristotle, and
ends with Adams,
Jefferson and
Washington.

Politics and
human nature
must seek good for
everyone and
creation of a good
political republic is
artfully Aristotle.

# Effecting

In passive air
soft spoken words
shaped minds
to see and hands
to write courage
like a composer
creating music from
instilled passion.

It was an amazing
transformation of
ideas into laws,
Washington like,
with humility
while seeking
greater good and
no reward.

It was making
something unique
from what materials
God provided,
not like a soft
teasing creek,
but more like a
raging river.

# Becoming

Humanity
rests
upon itself,
shoulder on
shoulder,
mind on
mind.
Every person
holds another,
stepping forward
with evolving
strides.
Time provides
birth and
death of
everything.
Hand in
hand,
step by step
humanity is
becoming
better or
worse, and
ultimately a
judging God
decides
human race
destiny.

# Weightiness

An idea has
no weight,
substance or
energy, yet
it has power and
meaning.
A man can think,
dream and
ponder past
today and into
tomorrow,
seeking new
ideas and
plans.
Shaping a
nation with
ideas is
evolutionary and
sometimes
revolutionary.
Every man,
woman and
child has
significance
beyond
self-awareness.
Humble ideas
grow beyond
imagination as
vision plants
seeds out of
which come
foliage and
fruit, and
new beginnings.

An idea is a
beginning of
awareness, a
zenith or
beginning of an
intention.
Everything
becomes
weighty in
one way or
another and at
one time or
another.
Weightiness
is only relative
to lifters,
thinkers and
leaders.
However,
aren't we all
lifters at
one time or
another,
pursuing a
pensive leader
with vision?

# Reasons

We wrote
opinions and
reasons,
supporting
decisions
made and
pledges
given, but
others had to
agree for
liberty to
succeed and a
new nation
to survive.
We created a
foundation
while seeking
support and
justification for
our actions.
We bled
hearts,
swallowed
pride and
vowed
lives with
no apologies.

# Republican Experiment

America is a vivid
continuum quilt of
diverse fabrics still
being sewn together
by divine providence
guided people.

Two inspiring
documents serve as
resilient thread of
enlightenment
for an indelible
faith comforter.

Declaration of
Independence
constantly pursues
freedom while
Constitution
guarantees rights.

Land and people
ever give America
substance and
material for an
exceptional
republican experiment.

# A Republic

A Republic is a
shared concern
based on
democratic ideas
perpetuated by
constitutional
representatives.

Oh, I can hear
Plato speaking of
his Republic and
Cicero and
Polybius
referring to their
Greek roots of
republicanism, but
mostly I hear
Thomas Jefferson
speaking through
words put on
novel paper and
approved by
many others with
their pledged
lives, fortunes and
sacred honor.

A Republic is a
shared concern
based on
democratic ideas
perpetuated by
constitutional
representatives.

Oh, I can feel
Jefferson's
weighty words
on my mind and
sense his
influencing
guarantees of
rights, and
am persuaded to
vote and be
represented in a
suspicious way for
I desire another
Washington to
stand tall and
point towards free
tomorrow with a
humble mind.

A Republic is a
shared concern
based on
democratic ideas
perpetuated by
constitutional
representatives.

# Natural Man

Within mind,
body and soul
rest humanity,
waiting for logic
in all its glory
to reveal natural
rights of all
human beings.

Earthly morality
quietly and calmly
holds hand of
mortals walking an
anxious path while
seeking wisdom
buried within their
heavenly spirits.

Justice seeks
sound reasoning,
commands humanity
to beget questions,
find answers and
naturally explore
innate benevolence
in quest for validity.

# Flowers

A natural
flower
knows itself
while existing
in oblivion,
for surely in
its limited way
everything
just is and
freely correct.
Inherently from
seed to seed,
pollen to pollen,
root to root,
nature seeks
own reasoning
means.
All rules are
subject to
evolution.
All means are
subject to
progress.
Flowers know
naturalness
without
awareness,
thinking,
reasoning or
judgment.
Truly, can a
human being
be less than a
flower?

# Change

Like bees
pollinating,
men planting
seeds or
rain melting
grimy snow—
change defeats
what was and
opens
promise for
what could be.

Existing is
good, but
sometimes
change is
better—
freedom
seeks good,
better and
unsurpassed
in time and
untamed space.

# Happiness

Evening light
creeps over
my world,
waning sun seems
unusually hot,
silhouetted beasts
roam grudgingly.
I hear them
speaking buffalo
as if a hundred
cooperative years
never happened.
I feel akin to
amazing earth as
Badlands spike
distant red sky.
I can taste
parched air,
mouth begs water.
I cannot
amply convey
striking beauty.
I am physically
happy as a
buffalo roaming
near plain.
I am spiritually
contented while
feeling God's
natural beauty
within my soul.

# Equality

It is yet hard to
understand all people
being created equal.
Inequality portends
its ugly self well.
And, do those few
unalienable rights
apply to everyone?
Oh, I believe in a
Grand Creator and
seek His help
because judgment
is coming alive
here in this
time and place.

Maybe we are all
equal under law, but
even that I question.
Maybe we are all
opportunity equal, but
that seems suspect.
Maybe liberty is an
attempt to strive for
natural justice and
lawful perfection.
It is yet hard to
accept all people
being created equal,
for I fear bigotry
is in our nature.

# Appealing Creeks

Man often
leaps narrow
illusory creeks,
stretches past
trepidation of
getting dirty,
feels anxiety
and humility
while leaving
vanity behind.

Soft mud
on either bank
slips underfoot,
threatening
bold decisions
while black ooze
silently sucks
confidence and
tries to impede
dreams.

Thankfully
pitfalls and
traps like
illusive creeks,
possess no
agendas or
disagreements,
letting strategic
man pursue
eclectic freedom.

Man constantly
falls onto
soiled knees in
apt position for
praying and
thanking while
over shoulder
he gazes at
slightly altered
leaped creeks.

Within stealthy
nature, however,
lies truth and
natural justice,
for undisturbed
creeks cannot
ignore man's leaps
nor can a nation
ignore choices and
indiscretions.

Thankfully
pitfalls and
traps like
illusive creeks,
possess no
agendas or
disagreements,
letting strategic
man pursue
eclectic freedom.

# Sovereignty

Sovereignty
used to
long skirt dance,
stepping and
prancing with
awkward motion,
but now new
dance steps are
required and
she falters a bit.

An old fiddler
teases strings and a
new banjo player is
learning how to flirt.
Even modest music
frees a man's mind
no matter its worth,
but excellence music
simply liberates a
natural man's soul.

Sovereignty is a
slow methodical
musical score making
love with a dancer,
and if truth be told,
sweet sovereignty
is becoming a
freedom-loving
ballerina performing
on a national stage.

# Liberator

I am like wind
moving with
biased meander.
My gallantry seeks
destination while
freedom demands
revolution for
expanding ideas.
Spirits sit on
my rounded
shoulders while
angels whisper
liberating thoughts.
Subjective wind
does blow with
purposeful resolve.
Like melancholy
music seducing
tomorrow's dreams,
I fearlessly
seek triumph and
command it be so.
I blusterously
wish to sing
songs written that
will become a
continuum of
distinct voices
crooning liberation.
Subjective wind
does blow with
purposeful resolve.

# Truth

In quiet realm
I sit with
hands folded,
remembering a
righteous man
speaking of reality.
He caused
me to think
about, "Truth,"
who has no
companion.
She sits out there
all alone on a
high hill with
morning breezes,
soaking rains and
evening sunsets.
Truth is a
lonely essence
waiting for cohorts.
Sweet time is
her measure and
process her result.
I unfold
my hands and
reach toward
heaven, for
inevitably truth
seeks my spirit,
life legitimacy and
collecting soul.

# Thoughts

Strange how thoughts
many times linger as if
they belong in mind,
growing to like it there,
wishing not another
enigmatic place to be.
They are mostly like white
doves, swarming mind,
soaring for attention.
Sometimes, however,
there are bad thoughts
being like weeds that need
hoeing and pulling, and
if left unattended die as
lost organic material.
Hopefully most
thoughts are good
like those soaring
white doves or like
blooming flowers.
Seems all thoughts
sooner or later
dry and in time decay,
but wisdom is gained
along time's way as
joy is shared and
thoughtful judgment
weighs lightly
like a dove soaring
in free selfless air.

# Chapter II
# Being Selected

# May 20, 2014 – 9:30

I found a chair on the south side of the deliberating room. Two big windows with open wooden louvers allowed light into the room, revealing clear blue sky. I decided it would be a great weather-wise spring day, seventy-two degrees and sunny. I, however, didn't wish to spend my day out there riding my motorcycle or drinking coffee while in my green metal swing. I didn't wish to surround myself with wife's flower garden or enjoy those plush trees exploding with new leaves. No, I wanted to be where I was, waiting to be selected for jury duty. I thought my chances were slim for selection; but I kept my mind open, just as I would if selected or while hearing evidence and finally placing judgment. I found myself in another world of which I knew not its nature. I sat waiting for someone to guide, educate and tell me what to do next. That soon came when a middle aged, but attractive black lady, the bailiff, arrived to explain Superior Court One.

I slipped into that unfamiliar world after answering her questions concerning my name and jury number. I loudly answered, "Phillip Reisner, #191," to let her know I was present. She checked her list and I instantly was put into her world.

I mentally reviewed what had taken place so far and the possibility of sitting in the jury box. Everything was mentally flashing like possible written chapters of an envisioned book to be later written.

The bailiff explained that she was the person we would rely on for guidance and also the one through whom we would communicate with the judge and the court. I listened carefully as she explained that thirteen people would enter the jury box first and the lawyers from both sides of the case would question us; the first thirteen were chosen by the lawyers based on questionnaires returned last year. They probably had a basic profile of each of us. They wished to further find out those things best suited for the prosecution and defense of the case. I planned on being selected, but for then I was just one of the first thirteen.

After the thirteen of us lined up outside the jury deliberation room and walked the hallway leading to the courtroom, we sat in the jury box waiting for more instructions. I lined up as the fifth person chosen out of the thirteen. The first lady in the line led us into the courtroom after hearing the bailiff say, "All rise."

It seemed like I had been waiting all morning outside the courthouse, waiting to go up the stairs, waiting in the deliberation room, waiting for my number to be called and waiting in line to enter the courtroom. I was anxious and excited, sitting in the jury box. I passed through two huge oak doors and walked humbly into the silent courtroom, past an oak railing, past two large tables where the lawyers for both sides stood and finally I stepped into the jury box to assess the courtroom. I felt like a very important part of a process about to take place.

I wondered how long the defendant had been waiting for this moment, how long the lawyers had been preparing for this moment and how long the judge had been waiting to try this case. I realized my wait was surely less than anyone else in the room. Hell, I waited a lot more in the Navy than on a beautiful day in May; surely the person who had the toughest wait of all was the defendant.

He sat seemingly relaxed at the table to my right of the courtroom. He was dressed in a khaki pair of pants and a striped polo shirt, and with uncombed hair. He appeared not interested in impressing anyone or maybe he simply didn't want to be anyone other than himself. I believed he truly felt he would be found innocent and willing to chance a favorable outcome through a jury trial.

It surely had been a long hard wait for him. "Oh, how I love freedom," I mentally remarked. "Oh, how the defendant must desire to remain free."

George Washington was a revolutionary hero and a man of integrity with a deep sense of duty, honor and patriotism. He was indispensable during the birth of our nation.

He, however, considered himself expendable when it came to importance of being president, thinking the cause of liberty was more important than any individual.

Surely the defendant had no sense of George Washington being present, but I felt his legacy in the courtroom, and the importance of the justice and jury system.

I applied those simple, powerful words given to us by the Founders. Washington believed in the radical idea that unprecedented power could be given to the people. Even little unimportant me felt the weight of decision. I couldn't imagine the weighty decisions George Washington must have made during his life. I learned about many things he did during his life, being the first president of the United States was probably the most important, but declining to be president again just might have been the most important decision he made. He didn't want to be like a king, yet many wished him to remain president.

I thought it remarkable how one person's decision could influence another's life so greatly. I was sort of in a George Washington situation, but of course in some tiny humble way. I, however, realized sometimes a decision might seem unimportant while it is yet very important. Of course decisions while serving on a jury probably seem unimportant to most, but it became very important to me.

My mind wandered as I sat in the jury box thinking about history, and about decisions and consequences. I thought about how this part of the country, Tippecanoe County, must have looked during the Washington years.

I recalled a huge wall painting on the first floor of the courthouse. The mural caused me to think about Lewis and Clark who ventured west from St. Louis shortly after Washington's time.

President Jefferson commissioned Captain Lewis and his close friend William Clark to explore the western part of the United

States in 1803. Jefferson asked them to find a practical route across the western half of the country. I thought about how hard it must have been and the tough decisions they must have made during that expedition. I knew the painting downstairs portrayed this part of the country, but I kept thinking about my recent trip to San Francisco aboard an Amtrak train that passed through the very territory Lewis and Clark explored.

It was a wonderful trip. Lewis and Clark must have had a magnificent report for Jefferson when they returned; they must have amazed him with their maps, sketches and journals. They must have awed him with their descriptions of the country. Their verbal metaphors must have been amazing, but I went beyond metaphors, I took digital pictures. I bet my pictures would have blown Washington's mind. I further wondered what he would have thought about the 3-D movie that was playing in my head as I sat there in the courtroom waiting for a trial by jury to take place.

# Whispering

I hear
whispering,
someone
suggesting that
insignificant me
should open
mind and
allow old ideas
to flourish.
Someone is
giving fresh
awareness
to old ideas
born thousands of
years ago.
I stretch
my confidence,
coaxing mind
to sense
pure essence while
melding ideas
into something
promising.
My inspired
American mind
understands that
few ideas are
truly new, but with
free thoughtful,
hammer and anvil,
I can forge malleable
providence.

# Glory Besets

An intrepid
eagle gracefully
soars above,
skimming
water surface a
long way
from home.

A naïve
fish swims
freely with
ignorance as
death waits
to snatch
fragile verve.

Fated eagle
with absolute
resolve
death shrieks,
seizes liberty
and causes
inequality.

Splendor is
assailed by
magnificence as
fated eagle
ascends with no
restrictions or
conscience.

# Wind Terms

Wind has no mind,
has one authority and
out of naive ambiance
sun creates a million
different winds daily.

No unique wind
is better or
worse than
another, yet
each breeds change
having naturally
bent essence.
Each divergent
air envelope
moves in
own appropriate
purposeful
approach.

Man, like wind,
is mysterious,
unpredictable and
fascinating.
No man has
authority over
another,
no matter
disposition.
No ambitious or
apathetic
man is better,
just different.

Both
quiet breeze and
scary tornado
seeks same
self-expressed
freedom.
All men are
same stuff
created and
must be
treated
thusly with
respect.

Contradictions
carry sacred
differences
into morning
breezes and
afternoon
storms with
natural desire.
Humanity is
impossible to
understand
even in simple
wind terms.

Wind has no mind,
has one authority and
out of naive ambiance
sun creates a million
different winds daily.

# Own Independence

Only I
know own
independence,
standing in
night air or
speaking to
Mother in
morning sun.
To me she
gave life and
will probably
not see me
elderly.
From her
womb
I came and
will ever save
her seed.
I am
liberated and
separated from
her, yet
our links shall
heaven find.
I ask, "are
all children
created equal?"
I am not sure,
knowing only
own bestowed
independence and
liberated self.

# New Thesis

An old man
quietly sits,
watching day
silently appear,
success being
morning
overwhelming
everything
with touching
sunlight.

Night is now
irrelevant,
pushed aside
in favor of sweet
day with all
her fingers and
toes displayed,
but no one is
counting,
only rejoicing.

A new day is
like a new
thesis declaring
freedom
for all, an
opportune
promise for life,
liberty and
pursuit of
happiness.

# Prosperity

Success is
like wheat
planted with
hopeful
toil, and
cannot escape
mindful
intentions.
It cannot
escape
harvesting and
eventual
processing.
Only early
summer days
answer
wheat's fate, as
evening
summer days
produce
bread making
outcomes.
True
success is
measured
one process
at a time.
True
prosperity is
pleasantly
eating simple
bread.

# Liberty

A group of men
touched a secret
mind place where
future encounters
silently hide, and
like a shadow
in a moon lit
courtyard,
liberty moved
slowly toward
courageous
illumination
seeking nimble
allure.

They mind
hurdled voids,
escaped limiting
thoughts,
pressed onward
towards
brilliance, and
elevated
themselves
like spirits and
gazed like angels
while delightfully
accepting future
liberating images.

# Bullying

I cry for
kids bullied
today,
especially
my friends
wishing only
friendship.
Father
talks about
intimidation.

Forefathers
wrote about it,
but I think
we forgot
much.
They said
we had a
right to be
free from
bullying.

Did they
also mean
little
insignificant
me?
Surely,
that's one
good
definition of
liberty?

# Salty Philosophy

Freedom slowly
unraveled as if a
rudderless boat
floating an
unfamiliar ocean,
silently escaping
coercion,
intimidation and
cruelty,
resolutely sailing.

It sailed from
white coastal
shores,
over endless
blue vastness,
whispering a
salty philosophy,
navigating a
majestic journey
to find America.

# Theory

Free ideas
surely wander
homeward for
they are more
than theory,
hypothesis or
belief.
They are living
soul burning
truthful torches
needing health,
wealth and
courage
kindling.
American minds
pave freedom
roadways.

Many have
truly explained
their need and
pledged
possessions,
lives and
honor.
American
liberty is an
accumulation of
ideas.
Western thought
continually
gathers toughly.
American minds
pave freedom
roadways.

# Malleable

To you
I give
hammer and
anvil.
Be
obligated to
use them.
Our future
seeks
strength.
Our past
revels
success.
I am
old and
skills are
fading.
Make
me
proud,
make
bellows
roar and
freedom
glow.
Life is
hard, so
make it
malleable,
help
shape it
well.

# Fermentation

Many
rejected
timidly and
chose
courage
over
coercion.

They
coveted
liberty
through
time,
space and
expansion.

Seeds
were surely
planted,
grown into
vines and
grapes got
created.

Aristotle
suggested
fermentation
long ago and
Jefferson
fashioned
true wine.

# Integrity

Some say
people are
morally corrupt,
knowing right
from wrong, but
unable to
administer
self-discipline.
Some say
people will
not respect
others' rights and
bring havoc
down on
everyone if
left in charge.
Others say
man's nature is
good and
he can
self-govern with
just a few rules.
Others say
education and
religion will
solve a new
nation's ills.
No one says
corruption and
disrespect is
good.
No one
wants a bully
next door.

# Courage

Oceans
remain
forever,
but heroes
aspire and
expire.

Earthly
blemishes
remain until
fear
defines
liberation.

Lonely
places
make
peace with
themselves
infrequently.

Friends
gather when
courage
flaunts its
protesting
head.

# Calm Water

Down a
certain path,
heading from
sure yesterday
towards timid
tomorrow, a
nation conquers
sand and rocks,
trees and grass.
Calm water
patiently waits in
silent meander
for pilgrims to
boldly live or
lastly die trying.

Cool
morning air
wrestles with
warm sunlight
reaching down,
portending an
aggressive pose,
seeking fog
burning fame,
knowing
everything is
changing as
pilgrims seek
foreign ways
to be free.

# Birth

No one has been
currently existing,
alongside creek's
meandering calm,
entering boat and
cautiously floating
uncertain domains,
modestly seeking a
peaceful separation.

Earnest thoughts
course through
water flowing past
stream banks and
human tissue
surging onto fields.
Warm rushing water
passes shoulder of
rejecting womb.

Learning how to
warily swim near
freedom while
mother screams as
flesh obliges and
seawater carries.
Mother arranges
natural birth and
God concurs.

# Akin to Trees

Akin to trees are
waiting rebels,
silently watching
their frightful
destruction;
cut down,
stripped and
hauled away
minus objection.
Black war
shadows make
streams
red flow and
winds burn
soul remnants.
Cold home
dirt accepts
brothers and
sisters young;
welcoming
those willing to
shed branches
and lay still,
marketing
themselves for a
wood worker's
decisive design.
They're felled as
strong, silent
children,
crafted into
lumber for
prearranged
promised coffins.

# War Begins with One

Turning heads and
averting eyes makes
ears averse to hear as
scorned minds of
burning thoughts
bare resolving truth.

Time gives way to
scared birds fleeing
as muskets boom,
collecting fear that
vilifies hearts and
alters calm doves to
dangerous hawks
along fearful way.

A republic begins
with one word as
people free fly with
concentrating eyes,
heaving minds and
collective ideas that
become organic,
truthful words and
wise sentences of a
rising declaration.

# A Bitter Pill

Authority
shouldn't
rule me and
make me
certain way
behave.
Authority is a
bitter pill to
swallow.
Maybe
authority
needs
my consent.
Oh, maybe
government
should
seek my
accord or
better yet,
my
permission
on certain
matters.
Yes,
government
should be
by,
for and
of people.
Oh, this is
simple.
This is a
sweet pill
to accept.

# Bread and Wine

Wind embraces
wheat fields,
vines hold
willing grapes,
ideas allow
minds and
souls freedom.

Some divine
power
entices men to
somehow possess
never-ending,
passionate,
horizon dreams.

Free beings
deserve right to
grind grain,
squeeze grapes and
feast on
life's bread and
wine.

# Free People

Cold rain
beats fresh
summer
leaves as
nature
rhythmically
drums with
thumping and
growling.
Ominous
falling
island clouds
slowly drift
freely towards
tomorrow.

People
nearly hear
laughter from
surrounding
forest trees as
they
accept
nature's gift.
Sun signals
storm's calm
retreat as
filtered light
seeks
people's
imagination.

People see new
forest rules and
regulations in
arching rainbow
grace.
Liberty is a
gold pot
waiting.
People
celebrate it
like childish
advocates
deciding
political rule is
yielding fate.

# Flower Basket

In a mental
basket I gather
beautiful and
haunting years
of memories
gathered like
muted flowers
screaming,
earlier heard
words rejoicing
their notorious
existence.

Over forearm
I gladly carry
enduring basket,
heavier and heavier
it becomes
to my delight.

My basket is
my soul, with
intricate spiritual
laced substance
heavenly formed,
God knows
basket making and
only He can
teach earthly
flower gathering
that verifies
my existence.

# Rights And

There are
three
God given
Rights and
ten
God given
Commandments.

Without
forgiveness,
there is
no hope and
only faith in
human nature
can save us.

Most
rights are
actually
privileges
granted by
people not
government.

There are
three
God given
Rights and
ten
God given
Commandments.

# School Buildings

A distinct
recalled place
built of stone,
glass and metal
would not leave
minds or
disappear with
new thoughts;
children listened,
teachers spoke,
utilities heated and
electrified while
young apprentices
came and went
to flourish in a
waiting world.

They became
builders, creators
warriors, inventers,
authors, teachers
mothers and fathers
pursuing culture as
traditions grew and
insight matured;
that school
building served
as an organic
structure for an
Indiana township
in a country of
hopeful children
self-liberating.

# Plight of Gulls

Flowers on
placid shores
arise and
quietly grow
from gull
carried seeds.
Nature loves
wind, rain and
obliging storms as
gulls surely carry
forthcoming seeds
past danger to
fragile shelters.
Such couriers are
not new and
seeds never tire
from waiting.
Silent seeds,
carried through
storms from a
thousands miles
years ago, yet
fulfill nature's
artful will.
Each seed lives
in poverty and
peace set to
germinate in
fragile destiny.
Gulls rest and
save their calling
in ageless days of
deciding time.

# Dry Wind

Dry wafting
morning air
carries sound of
bells clanging and
silently evaporating
dew drops on
brown latent grass
while exposing
accepted order of
vibrating change.

Dew drops
possess a
harmonic ear as a
church organ
reverberates
hallelujah music at
dawn and makes
trees dance to a
melody only
angels can hear.

Hauling wind and
nomadic dew
bond together
like a family,
making nature
send a message of
cooperation to
high plains and
low desert valleys
requiring rain.

# Chapter III

# *Judge's Instructions*

# May 20, 2014 – 9:40

I began to think my chance of being selected was pretty good as I looked around at other people, thinking about what I had studied, learned, accomplished and experienced in my life; also thinking I wouldn't mind if someone like me deliberated my innocence or guilt. I thought that person would judge fairly and come to a conclusion beyond reasonable doubt.

I was not a perfect child for sure, seriously rebelling against parents for about six months when sixteen. I was a good student, played basketball and generally behaved.

I studied business for two years in college, but didn't do well because of being interested in all subjects and deciding to learn by my terms and methods. I had so much fun learning that I forgot to study and thus I had a poor grade point average.

I joined the Naval Reserve because there was a draft in those days and the Viet Nam War loomed heavily on twenty-one year old men. I finally went on active duty for two years in Maryland and Germany. I traveled all around Europe and even got three Humanities credit hours after returning to college. I majored in Industrial Arts Education, that later became Industrial Technology, and graduated with a respectable GPA, getting all A's after returning from the Navy and applying some valuable lessons learned. I graduated in 1968.

I taught middle school at Crawfordsville, Indiana for seventeen years and coached basketball for twelve years. I also got married and had two children, remaining married for twelve years. The toughest thing I ever had to do up to that point in my life was leave my two children when getting a divorce. I left my wife, but I didn't leave my children. I cried often for several months, some after a year and once in a while after two years. I kept teaching for several years after my divorce.

I finally had enough of those wonderful little students and quit teaching. I did manufacturing, insurance sales, retail sales and remodeling of houses. I went back to teaching after a second marriage and becoming a father of twin daughters.

I ended my career teaching metal machining, construction, electricity, robotics, automation and CNC machining. Industrial

Technology was a far cry from teaching Industrial Arts at the beginning of my career; Industrial Arts included forging, foundry, lathe work and sheet metal fabricating. The computer entered my home, teaching and general way of life while out of teaching.

I had always written short stories and poems about spiritual, philosophical and experiential things. I began writing books about what inspired me after retirement and serving on a jury stirred authoring another book.

The judge of Superior Court 1 sat at his high bench surrounded by papers on his left, a computer at his right and a microphone directly in front of him. He watched while we filed into the courtroom, and when all were in the jury box, he said we could be seated. He started by explaining why we were there and what responsibilities we had according to the law. He further explained how things operated in his courtroom, and then introduced the court clerk and bailiff. He explained that the court no longer had a stenographer, but everything was recorded and later transcribed so there was no loss or misunderstanding concerning what took place.

The recording equipment was located in a small room near the front right side of the courtroom. He also explained that sometimes they, meaning him and the lawyers, would go into that room to discuss things not to be recorded. Some sidebars were to be conducted in that room along with other court needs. For instance, if someone had a personal or private reason for not being able to serve on the jury, the judge might listen to their reason in that room. A man of about thirty was called there with the lawyers before selection got started. He must have had a good reason for not serving because they all came out immediately and the judge released the man from duty. He quickly left the courtroom without a word.

The bailiff handed out a twelve page stapled pack of papers and we followed along while the judge read detailed instructions about the case. The bailiff collected them and we never saw them again until after entering the deliberating room; they were treated like evidence and we pored over them later looking for definitions and clarifications of the law.

The judge seemed mild-mannered, but stern; he later showed a sense of humor even though the case was serious to all present. I saw right away that he had control of the situation, control of his courtroom.

He introduced the lawyers on both sides of the case and then finally introduced the defendant. He referred to the bailiff as someone important to the court, how they had been together for several years and how she was of great help to him and the court.

Her domain seemed to be the whole courtroom, deliberating room and even the hallway leading to and from the courtroom. Her place in the courtroom was immediately to the judge's left. The recorder was at his right.

I very much hoped to be selected because everything seemed right; seemed to be falling into place, a twelve person jury and a criminal case. I was stepping into the judge's world, his domain, his freedom exercising space. He appeared to be a special kind of man, elected to a special kind of job, doing a special kind of work for the state of Indiana. And, there I was helping him do his job.

# Human Nature

Dust specks in a
dilapidated barn
are not signs of
uselessness and
deterioration, but
are like natural
spiritual particles
artfully floating
fearlessly,
revealing liberty
in real time.

And, within
degrading barn
conditions,
remnants of
splendor lingers,
inspired by
nature fashioning
itself as tiny
spirits floating in
restive sunlight
penetrating roof.

Evolving barns
seek history,
dignity and
beauty without
trying to change or
rebuild themselves
while accepting
unwavering,
natural essence as
dust particles.
Spirits floating

in free air
within a barn,
too soon come
to rest on
humble floors,
casually lowering
themselves as
unrestricted,
accumulated
communal dust.

Liberty is
like a continuum
of boundless
spiritual dirt
floating and
changing ever
so slowly,
changing artful
self-ruled calm
out of grubby
tyrannical rule.

# Strong Mind

A hungry
mind consumes
passion like a
violent river
swelling with
no regrets or a
coyote eating
sweet prairie
rabbits without
conscience.

A traveled
mind treats
life like a
cantilevered
structure,
levering and
balancing
as if being a
tall building
falling unafraid.

A forgetful
mind can
erase guilt and
mistakes like a
poorly written
sentence accepts
correction or an
eagle fearlessly
languishing
in airy myth.

# Strength

A piece of paper
speaks with
no conscience and
cannot consider
itself, but
he who writes
it can express
worldly ideas and
balance
principles over a
thousand years,
for one idea in
one document
can surely inspire
revolution.
Some write with
abundant zest,
weighting
truth and
justice with
partiality and
passion; but
he who
launches a
Decoration of
independence
is reaction
responsible,
for freedom
balances on a
fulcrum of
truth and
justice.

# Liberty Badges

To understand
protecting rights,
one must know
rights and to
know rights,
one must bravely
search history in
time and space;
for freedom dwells
loudly beneath
marching feet and
quietly within
respected graves.

To see one's naked
foot sole is to see
one's humble soul,
for freedom travels
by foot first,
then mouth, pen,
application and
finally safeguards.
Rights are often
trampled then
justly salvaged,
brushed off and
finally worn as
liberty badges.

# Three Questions

Can time fall on
rose buds well,
spread brilliant
petals through
nature's resolve to
unite moments
of day pausing?

Can we be
like rose buds
standing tall on
sturdy stems,
learn our way
towards sun in a
heavenly way?

Can we surely
provide beauty in
living days on
Earth's rich shell,
please eyes,
change moods,
let freedom live?

# Confederated

We feared not
for in our hearts
grace held
spirits and
souls taught us
to remember.
Time fed upon
itself while
solid thought
honed philosophy.
It was as if an
enlightened hand
reached down,
apprehended,
shook and
guided us into
political reality.
It pulled us
forward into a
hazardous
uncharted place
at a new world's
shaky edge and a
nation was
confederated.

o

George,
Tomas and
James yet warn
that power is a
precious thing and
sharing is
good government.

o

Representation is
wonderful and
judgment needed,
but an energetic
executive is
surely essential.
Oh, how should
it all begin and
operate fairly?
Maybe we need
something
more exact.
Thomas insists
on a new and
different constitution,
one for a nation
founded on
individual rights, and
power existing
with people, not
government.

# Someone Asked

Pain like
passion seeks
found love and
felt wounds,
both are
comparable and
compatible in
patient times.

Freedom
painfully seeks
dawn while
domination
plans for day
to end and
injure night in
hostile times.

Existence is
ordinary, but
particular folks
insistent that
passing time is
extraordinary
like sunlight in
gloomy times.

There are
some who wish
to make day
their own,
dominate and
make it
behave in
hostile times.

"Can't we all
share sunlight?"
Someone asked.
"Can't we all
be equal in
our chance to
engage it in
adoring times?"

"After all,
passion does
run deep and
often hurts, but
it's a personal
opportunity for
everyone in
liberating times."

# Nature Seems

Human nature
seems natural,
sewn by a
high powered
seamstress
bent on teaching
respect, love and
obedience while
clearly expecting
self-control.

Society crafts
rules as if life
is a game and
everyone will
play fairly, but
thing is, too
many folks are
naturally frail,
selfish and
dishonest.

And, who
will control and
encourage all to
sew a governing
quilt fairly so as
to help God's
creatures liberate
themselves and
embrace light while
rejecting darkness?

# Imperfect Beings

People named
stones settle
into soft dirt,
crisply washed
pant knees
get soiled from
prayer bending,
humanity gives
offerings and
apologies for
being imperfect.
A group of
stone carvers
make rules,
execute and
finally judge
others as if
stone is organic.
Human beings
bend and break
rules, faltering
because of
weakness and
vulnerability.
Stone carvers
come and go
while people
pray for moral
freedom with
bent knees in
clean pants,
silently reading
head-stones.

# Loud Words

Oh, Plato
I hear
your voice
speaking
nonsense,
saying
all men can
govern selves.
Most men
wish not to
climb such a
mountain, for
it requires
thought and
self-discipline.
Surely it takes
much time to
comprehend
democracy and
representation.
Surely it takes
conviction to
allow someone
else to represent
own interest.
Surely trust and
faith must speak
loud words to
manage individual
freedom and
factions alike
in a divergent
Republic.

# Inheritance

Inheritance speaks many languages,
earns attention and measures a
nation's assorted exceptionalism.

Accepted gifts give dimension to
unskilled souls, being good and better
together, making a nation excellent.

Freedom finds thoughtfulness,
principles and ideology, and causes a
philosophy to majestically burgeon.

Founders placed hopes and dreams
on a few precious organized pages
that remain long past manifestation.

Liberty now strives for tranquil history,
made in gritty development times while
mostly following brilliant Founder intent.

Like single morality, group ethics bind
exceptional American parts together as
inheritance today speaks many languages.

# Justice

Justice scatters rules,
regulations and laws
on a table as if little
sand grains gaining
civilized experience.
She's like an organic
judge and jury
seeking peaceful order.
She's a living entity,
enacting humanity;
ever scrapbooking,
teasing like a woman
seeking attention with
lawful regard for society.
She's for every citizen
expressing self with
written pages of clear
decisions while in an
enhancing robe
balances scaled facts.
She's a law definer,
servant collector,
experience keeper,
relic presenter and
decision maker.
She indicates and
finally determines
right from wrong.
She prosecutes and
liberates sand grains
on a constitutionally
assured desert of
free humanity.

# Diminishing

Justice shapes
time and space
like wind shapes an
ocean shoreline or a
courtroom affects
innocent or
guilty defendants.
Justice is
frequently a
shifter of sand, but
mostly a
manager of
majestic beaches
waiting tides.
Surf roaring,
boulders eroding,
decision making,
all are sand
becoming.
Justice comes to
all guilty and
innocent people;
like every stone
gets diminished
one way or
definite another.
Time and
justice eventually
hone and polish
every stone brought
to their hostile,
eroding attention.

# Peace

I seek peace
within bones,
down where
few penetrate.
I am isolated
in desire for
peace because
bullies and
thugs surround,
causing fear to
walk streets, much
less a dark ally

Peace won't
help when
conflict reigns.
Liberty won't
penetrates mind,
soul and spirit.
I cherish justice
more than peace.
I love liberty
more than life.
I'm ready
for a revolution.

# House of Words

They openly wrote words
well enough to create a
more perfect union to
establish an enduring,
permanent and
indissoluble house
for a new republic.
Their house had an
idea foundation,
rampart principles and
constitutional roof.
A founded republic
clearly housed a
growing nation of
diverse people with
strength enough to
lead a potent world.
They constructed a
house of words, a
republic of values
from lively argument,
They wrote plain for a
tyrannical king and
logical enough for all
freedom loving
colonists, settlers and
immigrants.

# Quiet Progression

My words
were ignored,
shelf placed as
eyes turned while
I verbalized a
future plan for
realization.

She was a
nation and I
her servant,
rubbing and
stroking her
with absurd
dawning plans.

I showed
her dawn
beyond glare,
exposed dusk
and revealed
night dreams of
reckless plots.

Some tried to
box me,
hammer and
nail me shut as
I floundered
with an army
of rebels.

Some sought
wealth, joy,
health and
then life, but
I dreamed of
endurance as
did a nation.

I recalled
black time,
yet projected
white time as
willing ears
heard and
active eyes saw.

I confidently
verbalized
new rules and
forgot tyranny
while seeking
liberty from a
distant shore.

My strong
United States of
America, surely
imparted liberty,
allowed dawning
sensibility and
begot a republic.

# Healing and Fixing

Healing values,
civil time and
much patience
like a tree
produced fruit,
spiritual men
found human
nature's covert
mending hand.

A steady hand
bore a nation's
milk and bread
for a while,
but crafting a
constitution
required many
hands making
sausage.

Decisions
sought destiny as
man's nature fed
America's fate,
mended faults and
fixed ethics, and
naturally valued
human nature's
temperament.

# Trusted Tripods

A mighty
distance exist
between
earth and
sky.
Nature
herself tastes
creeks and
rivers
where eager
wildlife
gather to
drink.

Nature is a
scabbard
protecting a
polished
sword that
slashes
hot veins of
three deer
carcasses
hanging
plumb on
trusted
tripods.

Rebellion lives
between a
man's feet and
head,
positioning
ideas on a
polarizing hill

in a place called
Freedom.
Three deer,
three tripods
seek equality and
justice.

A majority of
men considered
roaming into
thick far
woods to
kill deer
with enough
faith to
guide a nation
bent on
being forever
emancipated and
exceptional.

Aware
democratic men
pondered within
gentle minds,
used intellect to
exert reasoning and
allowed spirits
to apportion
historical wisdom
appropriate for
self-governing
words that came
naturally.

# Minority Rule

I'm like an
aware infant,
speaking and
thinking little,
but suspecting
big knowledge
that for certain
is far beyond
my capability.

I'm a fragile
nation feeling
prospects and
obstacles,
possessing a
hungry soul
for pursuing
wisdom and
knowledge.

My majority
maintains vines
while minority
eats grapes and
I'm afraid a
cruel drunk
will alter me
into a fruitless,
selfish regime.

# Fair Regime

I walk both
island shores,
wind and rain
in face and
against back.
I walk beaches
assisted and
repelled by
ever lecturing
natural forces.

I fear they are
weak and harsh
government parts
dictating life with
rule and control.
I wake mornings
wishing to repel
forces trying
to commandeer
freedom.

o

I wish to
balance three
island branches
of government,
with majority and
minority justly
represented, and
wish to invest
time on all three
island shores.

# Injustice

An unjust man
or faction
follows not
principles
imposed on
ordinary people.
A tyrant, majority
or even a minority
can succeed
with wholesale
liberty thievery.
Wrong behavior
becomes
acceptable only
when one or
many make
unjust rules for
weak others
not self.
Unjust regimes
don't follow
own rules but
boldly steal
freedom.
Civil body and
soul is unwarily
enslaved
when injustice
becomes
ordinary.

# Sweet Equality

Look deep
within heart,
take a breath
awhile or take
soul forever,
struggling for
correctness.

Allow mind to
write apparent
wisdom and
make everyone
gain a graceful,
warm liberation
philosophy.

Let hearts
know fitting
lawful words
enjoined to
allow wisdom
for freedom's
understanding.

Allow poetic
equality and
justice reign as
Articles of
Confederation
meld into a
Constitution.

Let brilliant
Thomas, and
Ben find
correct words,
because virtue
insists on
being present.

Let George
oversee
everything,
for good sense
is compulsory
in gathering
brave days.

A more
perfect union is
within grasp as
all strive for an
excellent and
meticulously
written promise.

# Chapter IV

# Courtroom

# May 20, 2014 – 10:00

I'm not sure if oak was extremely plentiful when the courthouse was built or if oak represented strength and endurance. Oak trees, however, are not the easiest trees to saw into lumber, carve with a tool or turn on a lathe. I would say both strength and endurance make sense because of all the oak present in the courthouse; it was symbolic and also plentiful in those days.

Whatever the reason, the whole place was filled with sawed, planed, shaped, carved, joined, turned, sanded and finished oak. My short journey towards the courtroom started with passing through double oak doors, then past dual oak tables for the lawyers and finally into the oak constructed jury box. I sat looking at jury box panels and the railing in front of me. I looked past the railing at the oak podium where the lawyers would stand and make their case and defend their client. I gazed at the massive oak bench where the judge sat and at both sides where the bailiff and recorder sat. I noted the large boxed space where witnesses would soon testify and try to build a case against the defendant. Large oak shutters attached to the oak framed windows blocked-out most of the plentiful sunlight trying to make its way into the courtroom.

The ceiling consisted of small white insulating panels with a one-half inch space separating their four by four foot size. I doubted if the ceiling was original, perhaps it was later installed for sound absorption purposes. It didn't seem compatible with the oak paneled walls and all the oak surroundings me. A large white screen hung from the ceiling for future media presentations.

There were microphones scattered everywhere except on the podium. The bailiff would move a microphone from a near table to the podium and back when needed to amplify a lawyer's voice. I later found out that she did this because the podium got moved out of the way during DVD presentations. The floor was covered wall to wall with gray carpet that captured sound.

I silently passed in and out of the courtroom often with my head bent downward looking at the carpet and not making eye contact with the lawyers or the defendant. I am not sure why I did that except to possibly not tip my hand, or give false readings about my disposition concerning the case. I also didn't want to be influenced by anything except the facts of the case.

I later found out that the law provides for personal experiences and beliefs. Maybe they knew my history. Of course the lawyers really knew little about any of us and that is why they questioned us about serving on the jury. I could not get over how quiet the courtroom was and how respectful everyone seemed to be towards the whole process. It was almost like a sacred place. Oh, I could nearly hear Thomas Jefferson speaking.

I silently sat in my chair surrounded by the oak enhanced jury box, waiting to be questioned. I sat in the number five seat. The prosecuting lawyer started with number one seated person and worked his way towards me. He had our previously submitted questionnaires laying on the podium in front of him while looking us in the eye for character hints and listening to our answering words for reasons to select or not select us for jury duty. He, however, explained not being chosen had nothing to do with our character or qualifications, but that each person must be considered as being right for each case. He asked some very pointed questions, some of which I was glad he didn't ask me. He only asked me one question having to do with my being able to serve. I said that I had been waiting all my life to serve and had never been selected. He moved onward past me quickly because

I think I had already been chosen from the information given on my questionnaire. I reasoned that maybe they did have a reasonable profile of me before I walked into the courtroom. Besides, I was the fifth person to be selected out of the first thirteen. I figured that I had a good chance of being selected as long as I didn't give some dumb answer to one of their questions.

I thought the defense lawyer was a little more interested in us than the prosecutor and asked tougher questions. He asked several questions of other potential jurors. He then got to me and asked about the concept of a person always being presumed innocent before found guilty. He spoke about it being the responsibility of the prosecution to make a powerful case and prove guilt of the defendant beyond a reasonable doubt.

He asked one person about the American flag placed in the corner of the courtroom. It hung on a pole about eight feet tall, draping the beautiful stars and stripes that majestically symbolized the reason why we were all there in the first place. He asked juror number eight how many stars were on the flag as he pointed to it. The juror answered, "Fifty." He asked how she knew or did she presume to know that there were fifty stars. He asked her again if she presumed there were fifty stars. She answered "yes" to presuming and why she had not questioned the number. He pointed out that it might be an antique flag from 1954 and that she would have been incorrect. He then asked if she would take someone else's word concerning the number of stars on the flag.

He also asked what if someone swore to counting them and signed a piece of paper swearing to exactly fifty stars being present. He went on to ask, "Would you believe that person and acknowledge beyond a reasonable doubt that there were fifty stars? She answer, "Yes." I mentally answer "yes" myself.

I answered strongly when the defense lawyer asked me about the innocence thing by saying that I thought it was something I just grew up believing, for instance when dealing with my father, and that I was innocent until someone proved me guilty. I wanted my father to assume my innocence, especially if it was my word against other kids, teachers or adults. Of course I was not always innocent and confessed to him. I grew up thinking my father would believe that I was innocent unless I was actually guilty. I was seldom guilty, but when guilty, I was willing to receive my punishment. I thought the defense lawyer liked my answer because he moved on to juror number six quickly.

Six of us were selected out of the first thirteen and that meant another thirteen had to be called to the jury box for questioning. We returned to the deliberation room and the bailiff told us how the process would continue. We later filed back into the courtroom and sat on the back row of the gallery while the next thirteen people were questioned. The lawyers selected six out of those thirteen people. The judge dismissed the seven not needed. He finally had twelve people to serve, yet needed an alternate. He picked four new people to step into the jury box. The lawyers questioned them slightly, and with little time spent, the judge chose an alternate. We recessed for lunch at about 1:00 pm. We were on our own to find lunch somewhere close to the courthouse.

We gathered in the deliberation room after lunch. I thought about the questions asked by the lawyers, reasons given for not being able to serve and answers given by several of the potential jurors. I was proud to have been selected and suspected why some of the people were not selected, but I honestly didn't understand why we, the final thirteen people, were selected as being best for this case. I later had even less of an idea why some of my fellow jurors were selected. The whole process was a mystery and yet it was working well and fairly. Of course that was my subjective opinion applied as objectively as possible. I finally sat in the number two juror seat, being juror number two.

# Power Separation

One
all powerful
person can
seek coercion.
Two
dominant
people can
seek power.
Three
commanding
people can
pursue equality.
But, a million
equal people
can insist on
freedom.
Sooner or
later,
however,
one
humble,
commanding
person must
lead with
prudent help.
One powerful,
commanding
yet humble
person must
occupy one
White House
oval office.

# Shimmering Lines

Good government
timidly traverses a
quivering line,
moving in an
unsure direction.

Experience and
advice glistens
brilliant minds
like sunlight off
rippling water.

Jagged idea
edges separate
real from false
impressions that
create images.

Lustrous views
seem artificial in a
shaky mind,
vacillating between
reality and idealism.

Perhaps
good government is
merely separating
images and recognizing
isolating lines.

# Publius

Publius first
spoke softly,
then gained
volume and
finally from
roof tops
shouted.

He often
opened doors,
parted walls and
found receptive
meetings to
philosophize and
provide advice.

He did not
wait until mobs
misread ideas and
ravaged logic, but
showed how to
dissent and
advocate freedom.

Publius actually
never spoke, but
Federalist Papers
were written by
authors Madison,
Hamilton and
Jay.

# James Madison

James Madison
is again
knocking at
doors.
He's always
selling an
idea or
explaining
reasons for
living free.
He can also
hear from
high places,
folks steadily
pounding on
his heavy
oak door.
Higher up
never means
lower
hearing for a
Founder.
James Madison
speaks about,
listens to and
helps write
federalist papers
day and night.

# Flowers and Ideas

In tight
holding hands,
flowers and
ideas wilt.
Strong
forceful
hands are
wonderful
when used
properly for
certain tasks.
Power
seems a
responsible,
educated,
managing thing.

What good are
powerful hands
minus humility?
What good is
responsibility
without good
judgment?
Flowers,
ideas and
regimes
need careful
tending and
profound
civilized,
natural
obedience.

# Engraving Power

In patient
hands,
power artfully
engraves
government,
like an
ocean's energy
impressively
carves
shore stone.
Creating a
constitution
requires
poise and
self-reflection.
It requires
balance of
power and
definition of
engraving
responsibility.
Power
separation is
three hands
balancing
obligation,
authority and
justice.
It's balancing
with Legislative,
Executive and
Judiciary hands.

# I'm Only a Barrier

I'm a
document
being born,
artfully written,
honed and
refined,
moving near
some zenith
distillation.

I'm
becoming
more refined,
my stature is
growing for
thinkers are
writing
unprecedented
principles.

Soon
I'll be
splendid and
unique,
not only a
barrier to
guile, but an
invitation for
artful action.

I'm moving
commonly,
gathering state
by willing state,
becoming an

evolving enigma
for something
greater than
any individual.

I shall
act on behalf
of all people,
not paper,
not power,
not a king's
decree, but a
constitution for a
thousand years.

# America

I shall
not be an
unnoticed
sand grain
recovered
on a beach.

I pray God
will deem
me time
after my
eroded stone
creation.

I cherish
Founders'
wisdom
written,
blessed and
experienced.

I am
liberty,
witnessed by
people,
gathered by
God.

I am an
idea, a
philosophy, a
republic,
I am America.

# River Power

Even though a
river has
boundaries,
it frequently
demonstrates
boundless
power,
becoming
unrestrained.
Rivers are warily
different, but
naturally similar.
Riverbanks,
dikes and
dams have few
valid self-control
motives and
means.
Necessary
man-made
means are to
prevent river
exploitation and
cruel behavior,
coming from
natural bents.
Security
needs powerful
water principles,
practices and
physical laws
understood.

# How Many Times

I sit vaguely
in a mixed
emotional state,
without reason,
without plan.
I silently and
mindlessly gaze
through large
lucid windows.
Cold rain drops
pierce morning air
like random bullets
seeking earth
without reason.

Temperature
suddenly creeps
downward as if
silently stalking rain
while a colorless
cold front pushes
gradually eastward.
Unaware rain
changes leisurely
into snow,
floating freely,
gracefully seeking
warmer earth to
helplessly melting.

Snow is briefly
beautiful for
it is again
splashing rain
falling hard

upon waiting
Earth's rigidity.
I am at times
like a changing
cold front, but
most times
I am like rain,
resisting radical
alteration.

But, I will soon
not sit remiss
with mixed
emotions,
no reason
or plan.
I will soon
address
my fellow
compatriots and
speak of
emancipation,
and unlawful
change.

# Table Reality

Civil reality
arose as a
sparkling idea
shared across a
big table where
Virginians
philosophized.
Truth found a
natural home
inspired like
flowing water.
Freedom hid
in murky water
within a
King's conceit,
yet liberty
surfaced from
two thousand
years of debate.
From gathered
minds a
man named
George Mason
emerged to
circumscribe
independence,
drafting a state
constitution
well enough
for a nation's
blueprint.

# Searching

Searching for
answers,
searching for
truth,
searching for
self-interest
is an endless
negotiation of a
reality quest
between
here-now and
then-there.
A freedom
plagued mind
cannot idle or
presume justice,
but constantly
refashion,
reorient and
clarify balance
between
bitter power and
sweet liberty.

# Liberty's Permission

I relaxed on a
wooden raft,
drifting southward,
in an inert state
called "flux."
I flowed
on water as a
weak legislator,
ignoring banks,
resisting sun,
forgetting current.
It seemed
I rode life's
course with few
scruples while
neglecting and
discouraging
dreams.

And then,
"We The People,"
exercised free will,
tamed an out of
control politician
as if he was a
raging river.
People became an
accomplishing
energy force that
threatened to
alter and
end my authority.
They sensed
worth and sought
permission to

meld liberty and
representation.

I recalled that
America is a
freedom raft
naturally drifting
on a benevolent
flowing river, and
I, their servant and
river look-out,
asked permission
to again be their
representative.
I was reminded
to never forget
that impressive
Declaration of
Independence and
that magnificent
Constitution.

# A Gardener

Even a gardener
dispenses honor and
humility like a
shadow casting itself
on a sunny morning.
And in darkness,
his judging shadow
faithfully remains.
He falls on knees,
when red lightening
severely flashes, and
prays for guidance
against nature's wrath.
Assaulting storms
threaten poise and
erode vigor against
mounting rebellion.
A good gardener
must not falter when
storms attack and
flowers and weeds
alike are watching.
He cannot cover
his watering eyes
out of shame as
overt integrity
protects against
unlawful storms.
True knowledge of
natural justice is
essential for moral
garden governance.

# Pin Point of Light

I felt potent words,
like rain on
bare skin beating.
They led me
onward through a
judiciary maze
where wilted lilies
languished and
silent water waited.

Questions arose and
carried me towards
some deep
intellectual place.
Mind sought
ethical words, but
silence prevailed.
I had no sound
place to go,
no firm one with
whom to speak.
I felt alone in a
forsaken pit.

Then above a
pinpoint of light
beckoned.
I heard,
"Climb towards,"
and I warily did.
Light filled eyes,
mind grabbed
craggy beliefs like
protruding stones
on a wall and

I climbed
warily upward,
little helped
me onward as
I rose higher
into brilliant
sunlight.

A different
kind of words
led me upward as
I followed a
different path
through a
different kind of
mind maze as if
those stones were
growing lilies and
flowing water
whispered
inspiring words.

Potent words,
were yet like
rain on bare skin,
but now caressing,
as I reached a
crescent edge and
freedom in a
judiciary maze.
I could now
pick lilies and
wash my face with
silent rain water.

# Three Branches

A Legislature must
find strength when
crafting ideas that
lie awkwardly in
storm's path and
with willful grace
reiterates rights and
responsibilities.

A skillful Executive
must surely reject
fragile laws,
make safe ones
behave and
renew faith in
constitutional
authenticity.

A fair Judicial
must surely act
like rearing a
child patiently and
with lawful bracing
as if a building,
three houses or a
whole free society.

# Three Valleys

At distance
government
branches like
three mountain
valleys look
peaceful and
attractive,
yet truthfully
all conceal
beastly dangers.

Checking and
balancing
safety never
diminishes
until reaching
majestic
mountain top.

Lofty grace
seeks and
finds guidance
for others
rather than self.

Jointly climbing
melds differences
into silent glory and
begets confidence,
satisfied with
fit truthfulness.

We live,
defy odds and
stake claim
on tomorrow,
whether,
walking a valley or
climbing a mountain.

Government
branches are
like valleys,
seeking own
rain and sun,
grass and trees, and
willing to share
views with any
mountain climber.

# One

One vigorous
three branch tree
is lacking unless
it has many limbs
shooting and
twigs meandering
towards sunlight,
becoming a lavish
forest of modest
trees providing
generous shade.

Can one be
satisfied with
one tree that
only provides
basic shade?

One huge tree
influences as
each branch
silently functions
jointly beyond
individual means,
acting as many
smaller trees
vitally providing
given right to
pursue happiness.

Can one be
satisfied with
one tree that
only provides
basic shade?

# Ambition

Ambition
is beating
undeveloped
souls and
enlightening
shadowy
minds.

Ambition
is elevating
success like a
rushing storm
stimulates
lightening to
cause thunder.

Motivation
is creating
ambition and
both counteract
naturally as a
cause and
effect tempest.

Ambition
is brewing
in a heating,
civil caldron as
warm ideas
successfully
taunt dreams.

# Enigmatic Minds

I am a logical entity with
complicated fantasies.
I am a confidence and
shortcomings dichotomy.
I was an intrepid diver
seeking freedom and order,
but now I am a republic
free style stroking equality.
I am more than a created
jigsaw puzzle waiting and
watching for reality or an
unimportant board game
capturing lost memories
in irregular cardboard.
I am more like a
gathering storm cloud,
blowing white snow and a
edgy brewing tornado
all wrapped into one
magnificent democracy.
I am a living breathing
philosophy driven republic
being fashioned not by a
few enigmatic minds,
but by many forthright,
revolutionary spirits.

# Private Interest

I've had times,
moderate and
calm, when
satisfaction and
contentment
steered my life.

I've had times
when misery
masked patience,
like a rose bush
deaf to own
captive leaves.

I've had times,
neglectful and
insecure,
like a candle
unaware of last
wind flicker.

I've had times
when badly
ignored,
like a lonely
love poem
waiting delivery.

# Rights Sentinel

Government
operates with
anticipation,
not expectation
as individuals
open endless
duty doors
when elected to
protect and
preserve
personal and
civil rights.

Government
officials should
act like sentinels
when defending
those things
assured by law,
asking many
questions,
soliciting many
answers and
making few
mistakes.

# Vigilant Mind

A vigilant
mind gathers
wisdom as time
melds rational
deliberation
while a thinking
person gently
collects wisdom
like a spider's
delicate web
lightly captures
contemplation.

A mind
softly journeys
between eclectic
divisions and
fractured cliffs
while desire for
understanding
often converges
with an inept
thoughtless body
that necessitates
self-control.

# Colors and Faiths

Man's nature
pursues rigid
schemes on
winding paths,
and humanity
seems selfish,
for intolerance
is problematic
and hostility
often deemed
enigmatic.

Magnificence
occurs within
people while
disorder and
viciousness
emerge amid
evil schemes.

Never has man
been allowed to
govern himself,
yet founders
philosophized,
fashioned and
established a
new liberating
constitution to
bolster humility
and self-control.

# Good Deed Awareness

A good deed
given with
self-awareness
is valued less
than one minus
elaboration or
recognition.

Life is less
if lived without
liberty and
illustration,
but shoddy if
shaped from
false thought,
knowledge and
philosophy.

Self- respect
is required for
genuine public
awareness for
one's humility
balances
actions on a
life fulcrum
while one's
evaluation is
left to others.

# Chapter V

# *Presenting Case*

# May 20, 2014 – 10:30

I sat in a comfortable chair that tilted and turned. I placed my arms on the padded arm rests for comfort, but couldn't find a place to rest my hands. I linked my fingers placed on lap while gazing straight forward into the prosecuting attorney's eyes while he spoke for Tippecanoe County and the state of Indiana. He was teaching basic principles of law, reminding us that one is innocent until proven guilty and that guilt must be proven beyond a reasonable doubt. He said that he was required to provide a powerful and convincing case against the man who was accused of solicitation of sex from a child less than fourteen years of age and solicitation of child pornography.

I sat with twelve other people, one being an alternate, in a comfortable metal and vinyl chair as a large digital clock displayed seconds, minutes and hours in bright red numbers. It was 01:32:29, but I was not hungry because I wished to listen and learn from the young, but experienced prosecuting lawyer. I was there for the first time in my seventy-three years of life, celebrating my birthday just a few days earlier. The other old man on the jury looked older than me, spoke of his age as if proud to yet be living in spite of his poor physical health. I didn't tell him my age; remembering again that people say I look young for my age. I think it has something to do with good genes, exercise and eating correctly. I, however, think sweets are health food.

The prosecuting attorney again spoke and pointed to the United States flag draped from a rod in the corner of the courtroom. He asked if we believed there were fifty stars on the flag. Most of us nodded as if we believed the flag had fifty stars. He asked us how we could trust that his count was indeed true by him just saying so without actually counting the stars. He went on to ask if we would trust someone swearing they had counted them and that there were indeed fifty stars present on the flag. Most of us nodded that we would believe a sworn testament concerning the number of stars. I really wanted to count those stars myself, especially if someone's life depended on an accurate number, but I didn't say so. I didn't think something like that would be necessary if someone's freedom depended on the number. I later wanted more information like star number or more evidence and proof. I didn't want to accept someone just telling me something was true; I had doubts, and I needed more evidence.

He continued for several minutes and finished his opening remarks by saying that the slightly heavy and sad looking man sitting at the right side table was guilty of the two charges being brought against him. He summarized by asking us to find him guilty beyond a reasonable doubt, and said that he would prove guilt as the trial continued.

The judge asked the defense attorney to come forward to give his opening remarks. He was a tall middle aged man with a goatee and a protruding belly. He sauntered toward the oak podium as if a bit tired. He gave the persona of a man who was not interested in defending the man sitting next to him at the defense table. My first assessment of him was incorrect as I found out later. He was very good at his job. He explained how he was not educated about the computer, internet and web sites. I later concluded that he was pretending to be technology ignorant like a fox. He said he was lacking in computer knowledge, but asked some pretty smart questions concerning detectives using the internet to find criminals. We had already gone through jury selection where he demonstrated prowess in the field of law. I started to like him and his sluggish mannerisms, slow speaking and relaxed persona.

He mentioned two charges against the defendant that consisted of child solicitation of sex from a child between the ages of 14 and 16 and solicitation of child pornography. Both crimes were mostly by use of the Internet. I am paraphrasing the exact wording of the charges, however, the judge read them aloud and we followed along from a printed version. We were not able to take the printed package of charges with us to the deliberation room, but the papers were there when we got back to the deliberation room. They were considered evidence. The prosecution went over the charges and laid out the case as interpreted by the state of Indiana. We later went over the charges and the meaning of nearly every pertinent word while deliberating.

The defense lawyer had a different interpretation of the application of the law, not the law itself because it was explicit in its definition; he was more interested in the application of the law. I kept an open mind while both men spoke about the relevance of the law and what would later be proven or disproven.

One thing that hit me pretty hard and made my reasoning easier was that only one side of the courtroom had to make a powerful case against the defendant and had to convince us, the jury, beyond a reasonable doubt that the defendant was guilty. That set the bar pretty high for the prosecution as far as I was concerned.

The defense lawyer said his client didn't have to prove anything or even defend himself. The burden of proof lay squarely in the hands of the prosecution. He was innocent until the prosecution proved otherwise.

I figured the whole process came down to the idea of justice, that a person must be found guilty or innocent of a crime and receive or not receive punishment for that crime. I later found out it is not as simple as I thought. Things are never really black or white. I was learning that the law itself is not black or white. It reads as if black or white, but it is mostly gray. I was learning that my thinking was also not black or white; learning that even our final decision would not be black or white and that justice is sometimes a tricky thing.

I recently took a trip to San Francisco and took a picture of Alcatraz. I was going to take the tour, but it was all booked up until after I was leaving San Francisco. I was anxious to see what it was like on the rock. I played basketball several times at the Terre Haute Federal prison when I was eighteen, right out of high school. It was not hard time like Alcatraz. I also played basketball at Putnamville State Prison one time which was hard time and some really bad dudes were incarcerated there. I never went back to Putnamville because it was just too scary. I just wanted to see famous Alcatraz prison, not play ball there on the rock.

I couldn't help but think about the defendant possibly ending up in some prison cell if found guilty. I didn't know what the punishment would be for his alleged crimes, but any jail time is bad time. I truly believed he was innocent until proven guilty. I wished not to learn enough evidence to find him guilty, but if we did find him guilty, I would not feel sorry for him doing jail time.

I guess the picture of Alcatraz in my head was a reminder of the gravity of my final decision concerning the defendant's future. I prayed the Holy Spirit would help me do my job correctly. Alcatraz was 1.5 miles away from where I stood when taking the picture; it, however, was a world away at one time for thousands of men, hopefully guilty of their crimes. I fear some might have known injustice. I prayed our defendant would find true justice.

Both lawyers completed their opening remarks; it being much like that seen on TV where both sides make sense. I've seen it where two people present their side of an argument with two completely different views. I seldom see how that is possible, but in any case they are passionate about their position. That kind of passion was presently absent in our courtroom. I figured passion would come later in the courtroom and possibly in the deliberation room.

# Oh, Justice

Oh, justice
you never
rush towards
some unknown
situation—
you're aware of
meaningful
moments and
eternal time.

Time seems
most days to
pass quickly
without notice—
it flows minus
known aim or
meddling,
ticking without
responsibility.

True justice,
however,
lingers in
hours of
focus—
it encourages
careful
thought and
obligation.

Some people
deviate time
without notice—
but no one
can diminish

honesty without
timely notice
of political
deceitfulness.

Constitutional
awareness can
charge minds
because justice
is tolerable—
it yet can make
one second an
interminable
heaven or hell.

Justice is a
friend that
breathes
fairness into
government—
it pledges
survival of
individual
civil rights.

# Doves and Willow Trees

Honorable
moments
drive security
towards some
stable reality
that seeks
answers,
wisdom and
fairness.

Limited
brain doves
hover and soar
rationally,
just like
willow trees
naturally
know how
far to bend.

Questions soar,
wisdom bends
while fairness
understands
natural rights,
like innocent
doves fly and
humble willow
trees bend.

# Surgeon Hands

Just below
regime surface,
working hearts
anxiously beat.

Well-placed
artful stitches
hold ideas
together with
clear American
political words
as if skillful
surgeon hands
fix them with
political tools.
Founders
pray as
they put
British flags
away and
fly red,
white and
blue ones
along with
triumphant
battle flags.
Politicians
blush while
congratulating
each other with
humility as
hope for a
new day dawns.

# Ship Portholes

Old memories
drifted through
countless
naturally
created minds.
America was
like a misused,
tormented
barn crumpling
onto and
into earth due to
recognized
British rule.
Raw artful
destruction,
through
weathering
time revealed
inherent
weaknesses and
strengths.

Founders began
repairing and
putting a
government
structure into
liberated order.
Endeavored
intellectual dreams
began flowing
inevitably again in
free American air.

Ben, George,
Thomas and
fifty-three other
brave patriots
signed a
Declaration of
Independence, and
did not forget
memories
handed down by
generations of
audacious,
pilgrims that
followed those
brave beings
who envisioned a
new world's
future through
ship portholes
nearly four hundred
years earlier.

# Deadlock

Savage wind cleaves
warped boards,
skeletal beams sway,
weakened integrity
struggles.

It is a temporary
deadlock between
Mother Nature and
man's nature to
plan and construct.
Gnarled metal,
bent forged hinges,
flap like ornaments
from an unforgiving
assault.
Rusty nails,
half melted away,
broken and useless,
hold bravely onto
shingles and siding.

It's a temporary
stalemate between
what is and
what will be.
Rotting and rusting
exposed barn
cannot resist time's
insistent destiny.
Dank stink of
water soaked soil and
lingering dust odor
reminds of past and
future melding

of construction
to destruction.

It's a temporary
gridlock that
promises progress or
at least some
kind of change.
Time cannot think,
plan and
build anything.
It can, however,
change everything,
often enhancing,
or diminishing,
but most times
destroying and
terminating.

# Egomaniac's Paradise

My house sits
on a high hill.
Folks come from
all parts to witness
sausage making of
awkward words
regarding processes.
Special existence
revelry makes a
slaughterhouse
patron famous.
Everyone gets an
elected seat and a
day in metaphorical
streaming sunlight.
There are few
windows, yet a
hundred walls.
There are no
classrooms, yet a
thousand teachers.
All who come here
have common
interests with
those left at home.
It is a visitor's
dreamland, a
practitioner's
delight and an
egomaniac's
paradise.

# I Am

I am collected
rose petals
scattered at a
wedding,
deformed wax
exploited to
seal a secret letter,
three initials
scribed in
gathered dust,
silent musical
notes in a
mislaid songbook,
lines in some
forgotten poem
read at a funeral.

I am placed
objects on a
sagging shelf
displaying esteem,
cleared space
saving time with
judicial will,
well separated
elements doing
natural things for
freedom loving
individuals,
asked questions,
pending answers,
made promises
to a nation.

# Tending Silt

Natural seeds
planted
await growth,
penetrate
earthly loam
in quest of
ancient
dominions,
hold more
knowledge
than can be
gained.

Natural seeds
create
innate
flowers.
Innate flowers
create
natural
seeds.

Rain on
hard shells
seeks inner
softness to
grow buried
grace in
humanity's
fields to
to effect
angel smiles
while tending
bitter silt.

Natural seeds
create
innate
flowers.
Innate flowers
create
natural
seeds.

Mankind
evidently has
good and bad
qualities,
citizens have
natural poising
traits, and a
strong society
influences
all individuals
to do good.

# Testing Ground

Take tasks
seriously with
courage for
beginning and
ending times are
frightening.

Presidential
years give
existence
meaning as
brief stay
expectations
seek time's
unraveling
protection of
liberty.
All must
be vigilant,
hearing both
friend and
opponent
providing
advice.

Wish a
peaceful place
today to
govern and
tomorrow to
support.

# People's Liberty

Essence floats in
ethical search for
truth and justice as
resolution and
peace hold hand,
leading and
inspiring me to
seek a bicameral
legislature acting as
unicameral.

A former way of
being governed will
soon be ignited and
reduced to ashes,
allowing weightless
American spirit to
unite omnipotent
counseling and
allow natural human
beliefs to flourish.

An agreeable
interlude will
cause matter to
be dust again as
I indeed pledge
in tough times,
life, fortune and
sacred honor for
liberty and
emancipation.

# Legislative Art

I've had
six years,
fragrant and
joyful, when
intoxicating
truth and
justice
baked bread
enough to
feed my soul.
I've had
time to
craft and
count
legislative
blessings
while serving
passionately
as a Senator.
My soul
yet reaches
for grace,
tolerance and
freedom.
I've learned
legislative art
by being free
to exercise
people's will
for fair
governance.

# Being and Guiding

Be amongst
willow trees,
instinctively
engender
mild honor.

Be ever
nourishing to
aware minds,
inspire
calm justice.

Executively
bend and
humbly sway,
lawfully draw
creative water.

# Grain

There are
upset citizens,
indisposed,
seemingly life
betrayed like
wheat strewn
on a stone
path to dry,
die and be
windswept.

We might
find ourselves
like grain
injustice willing,
eager to disown,
surrender to a
tyranny and
think too much
inequality is
really justified.

One
grain matures
into fifty,
fifty into a
thousand, and
so onward goes
life's miraculous
advancement if
free to produce
and succeed.

o

There's a
fourth branch
ever cherishing
freedom,
wisdom and
knowledge,
waiting to define
lawful sense, a
branch willing to
find justice.

Supreme Court
judges assess,
but people are
fourth branch
who ultimately,
firmly thrash
societal wheat,
lawfully
govern bread and
feed citizens.

One
grain matures
into fifty,
fifty into a
thousand, and
so onward goes
life's miraculous
advancement as
branches grow a
republic tree.

# Sharing Freedom

I never thought
regime fidelity was
special until infidelity
consumed my life.
Little injustices
became important,
big ones made
me angry and
caused thinking
about my future.
I wondered if
too little liberty
might alter
my religion and
instinctively
make me
pray for it.
I questioned
whether lack of
freedom might
consume
my existence and
cause me to make
new friends or
fight a war for it.
I trusted that
fighting for
precious freedom
wouldn't make
me a fanatic,
but it surely did.

# Slippery Slope

Some time ago
I bravely placed
my ears on a
slippery slope.
I faintly heard
Mother Nature
whimper and
then whisper;
she revealed things
I should have
already known,
things like resisting
injustice, tyranny,
inequality and
pure wickedness.
I perceived her
speaking of citizens
being ignorant of
own government.
She then exposed
knowledge from
another time and
place; an ancient,
intellectual place
where philosophy
grew wisdom like
delicious fruit.
I couldn't help
but gorge myself
on thoughtful
freedom and
self-determination
delight.

# Chapter VI

# Witnesses

# May 20, 2014 – 11:00

There were only two witnesses for the prosecution that worked the Internet crime division of the Lafayette police department. I think they call it cyber-crime these days, but I guessed these guys just worked on crimes against children. The officer that actually communicated with the defendant, by way of the Internet, presented evidence of wrong-doing first by showing exchanged emails between himself and the defendant.

The defendant had originally sent an email on "Craigslist" soliciting what he called freaky sex and claimed that he was up for anything freaky. Apparently the officer routinely scanned several web-sites to find predators, pedophiles and deviant sex solicitation directed towards minors. One of the detectives came across the particular email and responded to it by pretending to be a fourteen year old girl. The defendant asked after three or four emails how old the person was on the other end of the conversation. The officer answered that he was fourteen. The detective said that he was ready, willing and able to give him all he sexually wanted. The defendant said he didn't believe that she was fourteen because he was on a web-site for eighteen and above age people. He, however, foolishly continued to communicate. He finally agreed to meet at the Dollar General parking lot at 12:00 pm before he went to work at 3:00 pm.

The officer and five other policemen were waiting for him at the parking lot. The defendant arrived, then drove away, saying that he did not see anyone, but then returned. At that time the police took him into custody for questioning. They did not arrest him, but said they only wanted to question him. It was cold that night in February so they took him immediately to the police station for questioning. Apparently the defendant never suspected wrong doing on his or their part and went willingly to the station. He was docile and willing to talk about any and everything as shown later on a DVD.

We took a break for lunch. I ate a sandwich and drank a glass of water at a nearby restaurant and spent $11 of my $40 pay for serving, and hadn't even been chosen. I gladly spent the $11.

The second witness testified that he had indeed questioned the defendant and that the defendant had answered all questions. The detective, however, insisted that the defendant knew the girl on the other end of the email conversation was fourteen. The first witness who was the persona character, said he was fourteen, but the defendant never acknowledged that fact. The prosecution showed a DVD of the defendant answering all questions honestly. The detective admitted that the defendant answered all question honestly and was totally cooperative. I thought at the time that the defense should have shown the DVD instead of the prosecution. The DVD seemed to sway my opinion in favor of the defendant.

The defense attorney quizzed both witnesses with direct questions. The first officer did very well answering the questions, but the second one finally was lost for words when asked, "Did the defendant answer all questions honestly?" He answered, "Yes." The defense attorney stated several times that the defendant answered all question honestly, but the witnessing officer insisted that the defendant lied about knowing the age of the fourteen year old girl. I think we were all surprised to hear him assess the honesty of the defendant as nearly impeccable.

The defense had no witnesses. It was about 4:00 pm by the time the prosecution was finished with presenting their case. The judge said we would recess and come back at 9:30 am the next day. It had been a long day, but I was not aware of passing time until the judge said, "Go home." I had forgotten about the bright red digital clock. Time passed quickly and I felt we had gotten a lot accomplished. My mind was saturated with law education, philosophy and procedure, and saturated with case facts and information; it was awhirl with verbal and visual information, and inundated with thought and reasoning. I couldn't help but begin to be, even though not supposed to be, sway towards one side as I attempted to remain impartial.

The judge told us not to watch local TV or read any local newspapers the next morning. He said he didn't see any media present in the courtroom, but didn't want us to be swayed by outside opinions and should keep our mind on the facts of the case presented in the courtroom. He said for us to not discuss the case with anyone at home.

I later spoke to my wife about the process of jury selection, how the courtroom appeared and about how the lawyers presented themselves. She understood my being unable to speak about the case yet was very interested. She figured that I had been selected because

I didn't come home early in the day. She was anxious and curious to hear about what had taken place during my day.

I pictured myself back in the courtroom, sitting in jury chair number two and thinking about the case and what had happened during the day; mind remaining awhirl until about 11:00 pm. I didn't sleep well that night and got up early the next morning even though I didn't have to be in the deliberating room until 9:30. The whole process of trial by one's peers fascinated me and I was slowly becoming more and more aware of personal responsibility. A man's life and his freedom was partially in my hands, maybe completely in my hands if I was the lone person to decide innocence or guilt. We finally entered the courtroom.

I kept wondering what the defense lawyer would say and what he could do to sway us towards his point of view. I kept playing mental movies over and over in my mind about what took place in the courtroom the day before. I was totally involved. Little outside of the courtroom seemed to matter while seeking justice and anticipating judging a man and finding him either guilty or innocent beyond a reasonable doubt.

The DVD was recorded from a high placed camera in a small narrow white room at the police station. One of the officers sat at a table with the defendant while the other officer, the one who had actually pretended to be the personae character, sat nearby in a chair pushed against a wall. The defendant was to my left, facing the camera, while the officer sat to my right with his back to the camera. Everyone was relaxed, agreeing that it was much warmer in the police station than outside on the Dollar General parking lot.

The questioning officer said the man in the room with him, the suspect, was not under arrest, but only there to answer some questions and to help them with a problem. The suspect was docile and cooperative. They all seemed to be friends. All that was missing was a couple of beers. The officer talked with the suspect about general personal things like his family, work and residence. He finally got to why they were actually there in that place, finally got around to talking about communicating on the Internet. The suspect openly admitted to having been on "Craigslist" and sending what both considered off color emails, "freaky emails," in the words of the suspect. The detective ultimately got down to the girl's age with whom the suspect had been communicating. He never mentioned that the girl was actually a police officer.

The suspect never admitted to believing she was a fourteen year old girl. The officer had tried to convince the suspect of that fact during the emails, but the suspect never admitted to that supposition. The DVD ended with the office saying the girl with whom he had been communicating was a fourteen year old girl and that he was in trouble for soliciting sex by agreeing to meet her and by asking for a picture of her "pussy." The defendant said he was only asking for proof of her age, thinking a fourteen year old girl would not respond to the picture request.

The officer didn't respond and never sent a picture, but the defendant did agree to meet at the parking lot. The DVD allowed us to see an honest man who had probably made a mistake by emailing for sex and he should have ended his pursuit when questionable age surfaced. I, however, never was convinced he believed the personae girl was fourteen. The DVD better served the defense.

It seemed reasonable to me that the police should have followed through with an officer that looked close to fourteen. I thought if the defendant had actually picked-up an officer thinking she was fourteen and drove off in his car with her, he should have been arrested and put in jail. I figured the police were lazy and thought they had a strong case and didn't want to take it any further. I would have had no sympathy for the defendant if he had picked-up the pretend fourteen year old, but instead I had sympathy for him for being stupid and foolish, and for being duped by a professional Internet detective pretending to be a personae minor.

# Truth Worthy

Minds hurdled voids,
thoughts resides and
ideas coalesce where
freedom elevates truth;
spirits selflessly share
ideas while angels
encourage decisions.

Liberated seeds
rooted in reality's toil
accept aggressiveness;
they get machine-
beaten, oven-baked,
Picasso-painted,
Adams-fermented.

Men sojourn
like seeds and ships,
planting soil and
growing ideas,
philosophically
baking and creating a
United States.

# Now Is Then Again

A naturally
open mental
gate exposes old
melodies from
intervening
lost days in
curious heads,
causing various
life reflections.

Melancholy
pictures of true
natural beings
fill curious mind
with crude
drawings placed
carelessly as
time speaks and
history repeats.

Human nature is
knowable and
predictable as
people try to
understand it by
living, forgiving,
controlling and
passing it to
future generations.

o

Past ways are
now again and
persistently,
ignorantly and
foolishly
reappearing.

Wisdom
sheds light
to educate
human beings
well enough
to be natural.

One cannot
relive or
revive past,
yet it haunts
like an angel
shoulder-sitting.

One must
listen to old
melodies,
dance and
invent steps to
live with self.

# Free Mind

In a secluded
mind corner
lives a speck of
divinity,
put there by
God in every
human being
since time's
beginning.
He caused
man to be and
share a
free mind.
Some say a
free mind
learns through
revelation while
others speak of
reason.
God's natural
free mind
reveals itself
through his
natural mind.
Liberty is a
holy thing to be
exercised by
human beings.
It is something
worthy of
fighting and
dying for as
so many have
executed.

# Reason

Miracles
go against
reason, and
reason is
enlightenment's
centerpiece.
Natural law
seems
reasonable, for
in nature
answers are
found, yet
revelation
seeks
attention and
respect.
God seeks
balance
naturally
between
man and
Earth.
Reason and
revelation
seem
conflicting, but
believers
freely
consider
own
natural
interdicting.

# Wall Between

A constitutional
wall between
church and
state exist
with a good
conscience
gauge.
Jefferson said
it so.
Religion
stands
protected by
law
along with
conscience
rights.
A common
Creator
bestows rights
higher than
earthly
realms.
He speaks
louder than
any state or
nation.

# Grind

We accepted a
miller's simple
idea of
grinding and
pulverizing,
changing grain
into flour.
We thought with
rough minds to
grind ideas and
make something
advantageous,
wholesome and
warm baked.

We grew ideas,
converted,
gathered and
compiled
them into a
philosophy, a
political
foundation.
We became
stone wheel
grinders with
no regard for
reputation or
safety.

Freedom
seemed a worthy
endeavor and
it grew within
limitless

crafted ideas;
where all
had a chance
to nurture,
gather and
grind wheat.
Wheat grinding
gave all an
opportunity.

Life,
liberty and
pursuit of
happiness
became goals.
Grinding
became an
honest and
competent
baking art.
Governing
became an
endowing of
future talent.

# First Duty

Please
don't crush
my warm
religion and
smash
my fragile
ideas about
God.
My first
duty is to
Him and
then to
my free
exercise of
religion.
Treat me
fairly,
no matter
my faith, and
within human
radiance, find
protection for
religious
liberty.
Let light
seek truth and
darkness require
spiritual glow.
Let tolerance
prevail and
bigotry find
enlightenment.

# Gardens

Virtue teaches and
seeks victory
like an accepting
moral nation
modifies people's
behavior for
their survival.
Virtue fractures
voters selecting
representatives
if acute crevices
erode honor.
Virtue allows
mortal flowers
to develop as
they mature.

Religion binds
people together
wishing virtue,
like cultivated
garden
flowers and
foliage,
collect sunlight.
Government
gardens
must surely be
cultivated
naturally for
God's eye and
divine nature
is watching.

# Liberty Roams and Soars

Religious liberty
roams a republic
weakly if most
fragile citizens
ineptly cling to
existing power.
Tenuous voters
naturally find
ignorance and
deep depravity
when eluding
responsibility.

God's piece in
each follower
bleeds easily as
impurity stains
blessed essence.

Knowing
faithful self
teaches truth
while accepting
accountability as
freedom initiates
frail spirituality.
Religious liberty
ascends lofty
mountains and
treks deep valleys
to find security.

God's piece in
each follower
bleeds easily as
impurity stains
blessed essence.

# Writing Sojourn

A Republic can
stub its toe
on civil and
religious liberty
even while
on a successful
constitutional
writing sojourn.
Dreams can be
nightmares and
plans wash to sea
if caution relents.
Principles and a
new constitution
build civil and
religious liberty.
Treading water
cannot protect
freedom from a
king's revenge,
but swimming
across an ocean can.
Writing a militant
United States
constitution is
like swimming a
risky, hazardous
Atlantic ocean
with head just
above water while
daringly stroking.

# Purview

Like rain
on parchment,
sweat stains and
watermarks a
possible
constitution.
Founder's
cannot escape
religious
concerns.
They gaze,
wrinkle brows and
clench jaws.
They wrestle with
tolerance in
religious matters.
They hear
understandable
questions
concerning a
nation's opinions.
Spirits rise as
consensus
melds beliefs
into considered
novel opinions.
They resolve
religious tests and
illegitimate
constitutional
tolerances to ensure
religious equality
to all people.

# Encouragement

An amazing cloud
drifts over earth,
knowledge droplets
descend towards
thirsty children
waiting wisdom
from edifying
atmosphere.
Thus begins an
adventure for those
who recognize
opportunity as if
omnipotent God
surely observes.

All agree that
accumulating
knowledge is a
noble work to
be encouraged.
Each citizen is
entitled to a
sound education.
It is as if heaven's
flawless grace
begins and ends
with encouragement
by principles for
American success.

# Pilgrim Monument

Eyes feasted on
Atlantic coast.
Nature headed
towards a novel
promising future.
Rain drops like
historical spirits
descended as
future needed
no support to
begin a dream.
Hope mindfully
awakened essence.
It was as if that
yet to be found
Plymouth Rock
spoke with whetted
awareness.
That place and
time was a
Pilgrim moment
to be ever
remembered.
A diligently
religious and
moral pilgrim
monument was
created from
ideas and
courage.

# New World

Clouds delicately hung
over distant mountains
like ghosts pleading for
needed attention while
unknown vanity and
known beauty drench
near valley with crucial
phantom rain drops
correctly seen as grace.

A new world teased
innocent eyes and
indulgent hearts
while harsh reality
threatened new
philosophies and
principles with a
diverse gathering of
political investors.

Time delicately
encouraged superb
spirits to reform,
ghostly rain kisses
touched mountains
life initiated westward,
unspoiled strategies
naturally shaping
new world grandeur.

# Artful Stone Wall

Accepting hands are
yet building a stone wall
between church and
state as if judicial grit
is building blocks of
abundant time material.
In some known way
it is being artfully
built and engraved
well enough to cause
frequent pause and
loving reflection.
It's an artfully shaped
wall that will never
realize its zenith, for
instead of people
honing it smaller,
they are increasing
its ultimate size by
just diversity and
verified rights.
Government is
constitutionally
striving to separate
church and state by
building a wall of
politics and religion.
Suspicious minds are
increasing grasp of
solid ideas through
elections and decisions,
thus separating and
building a stone wall is
ever an artful process.

# Mending Hand

America has a
broken hand
grasping in pain,
enduring time and
throbbing with each
soft tick of an old
informative clock.
That altered clock is
unique America
being rejected and
disrespected.
Freedom fighting and
Republic-clock-repairing
is a tough business.
Treating agony of a
broken government
requires more than
courage to fix a hand or
mend a distorted face.
It requires feasting on
selfless freedom of
historical time and
good management of
sovereign tools
in future time.
Freedom fighting and
Republic-clock-repairing
is a tough business.

# Imagery

Polite religious
imagery
does not
oppose words
concerning
constitutional
rights.
No gracious
design in a
public square
goes against
any law.
Well chosen
lexis informs
citizens with a
fair and
equal touch.
Anyone
can speak,
act and
share a
message of
his or her
own.
Unintended
kindness is
like brilliance
by accident,
it provides a
gentle way
to be human
minus effort or
preparation.

# Self-Control

True conscience
brushes mind to
cast shadows on
bad judgment.
Principles are
like rain drops
in a stormy life,
they cleanse
wrongdoings
when no one
is looking.
Sacred action
waters eyes and
brings sinners
to their knees.
Ethical storms
affect body,
mind and
soul, and
align with a
rebelling
conscience.

# Chapter VII

# *Deliberation*

# May 20, 2014 – 2:15

The defense lawyer stood after the judge asked him if he was ready to present his defense. He softly said, "The defense rests." I was surprised as probably many others in the courtroom about his decision, but after thinking about it, he had presented a pretty good defense the day before when cross-examining the two witnesses. He had asked the right questions in my opinion.

A juror can ask a question of a witness, presented in writing to the judge while the witness is yet on the stand. The judge then reads the questions just as they are written. I had written a question on my notepad concerning why the police had not confiscated the defendant's home computer, but the defense lawyer asked the question during his cross-examination of the second witness. The police officer, on the witness stand, admitted that they believed the defendant had nothing on his computer concerning child pornography and the conclusion was based on what the defendant had told them during interrogation. He admitted to believing the defendant had been totally truthful at that time, except of course for him not admitting to believing the girl on the other end of the line was fourteen. There was also nothing on his phone to indicate any child pornography. I didn't submit my question to the judge because I got the answer during cross-examination.

We were ready to hear lawyer summations from both sides of the case. The prosecution reiterated our obligation to determine the defendant's fate with a candid mind and to finally decide both verdicts beyond a reasonable doubt. He recapped the evidence by hammering away at the emails that supposedly showed intent to do the crimes. Intent was a nebulous term to me. I found it difficult to believe the man was guilty of soliciting sex and pornography from a minor when he didn't actually think she was fourteen. The prosecutor seemed to be putting all his eggs in one basket and had not done enough work or collected enough evidence to make his case. He soon rested his case. Even though he was a good lawyer, he just didn't have enough evidence in my opinion. I was certainly leaning towards not guilty.

The defense lawyer sauntered towards the podium, and with found energy soon got to the point of convincing us that his client was innocent. He repeated that the emails showed his client never admitted to knowing the girl was a fourteen-year-old. He said his client didn't even know if the person was white or black, male or female much less under-age. The officer admitted the man interrogated nearly never lied. He, however, believed the defendant lied about one thing and only one thing, and that being the girl's age. I found it difficult to believe the defendant lied about only one out of a hundred questions.

The defense lawyer looked directly into my eyes several times, maybe because I was directly in his view or maybe he reasoned I would believe his client was innocent later during deliberation. Either way, I connected with him and probably tipped my hand concerning the trial by looking at him in the eyes. He concluded his defense by lecturing us again about reasonable doubt and one being innocent until found guilty. He and I were on the same wave-length.

The judge read and we followed along from a typed package of court instructions that would help us during deliberation.

"All rise," the bailiff said loudly. We slowly filed out of the jury box, second row first and then my row. We passed in front of the two big lawyer tables. I yet gazed downward avoiding eye contact with the lawyers and then passed through the double oak courtroom doors. We walked through the hallway leading to the deliberation room where we had begun our day with thirty-seven other people sitting around a table and the room perimeter.

We all found a place to sit around the big five by twenty-foot table. I had more questions than opinions, but that was all about to change. Someone asked the bailiff how we went about selecting a foreman and she had little advice.

We were out there in so called "no man's land," or to be politically correct, "no person's land," because no one had previously served jury duty and thus deliberated a case before. The first thing I learned was that there is no longer a foreman of the jury, there is a foreperson. That was a subtle piece of knowledge gained from the bailiff. We all sat quietly while considering what came next and how we would select a foreperson without any information concerning those sitting around the table. A lady at my left spoke up first, nominating another lady who sat across from me. Apparently they had gotten to know each other during our short time together before jury selection. She said she thought that particular lady would make a good foreperson. No one had any objection or had another person they wished to nominate. The prospective foreperson spoke up quickly saying she didn't mind taking the job, but if someone else wanted it they were welcome to it. She said this while pulling out a yellow notepad and pen, placing them before her on the table with enthusiasm. No one spoke or suggested another for foreperson.

She immediately asked if we wanted to talk about the case or take a preliminary vote. I, along with others, said we would like to talk about it first. We had a short non-committal discussion, but I could sense people leaning one way other another concerning judgment right away. The foreperson said "Ok" after we went around the table while a few of us spoke, "Let's take a vote."

She spoke first by declaring her vote was "guilty." I couldn't believe she voted first and with such conviction. We continued around the table; the final vote came to nine people voting for guilty and three of us believing the defendant was innocent. The foreperson was surprised to hear the not guilty votes. She had strongly made up her mind and could not see any other position. I and the young lady sitting at table seat number one voted innocent. The older man to my right also voted innocent.

I looked around the old oak darkened varnished yet shiny table. Small drawers with old brass pulls were beneath the thick top on which I placed my hands. My future cohort in verbal battle sat in the first chair on my side of the table. I called her "First Lady." She was about thirty-five years of age, fit and attractive. I looked into her clear blue eyes several times and exchanged determined looks of commitment. I heard her say to someone else that she had studied criminal justice for two years, but I had no idea what she presently did as a career. I thought she must have been in some kind of business management. She certainly presented herself as very business-like while expressing her position well and being unafraid to share principles. I trusted her opinions.

First Lady began to go head to head with the foreperson of the jury early in our deliberation. I gained a great deal of respect for her as she spoke directly about what was also my position concerning the defendant; we were both certain where each other stood regarding the defendant's innocence. There was no doubt that we were thinking alike, speaking alike and willing to go to bat for the defendant alike. There was much non-verbal communication between us while verbally letting our positions known to the other people serving on the jury. It was strange how two people were drawn together to work on a particular mission while knowing nothing about each other. This task of saving a man's normal life was bonding us for only one purpose, justice. I figured we would never see each other again after the trial, but for now we were partners, cohorts, worriers.

The next juror in the second seat around the table was a small young woman who was irritated about being selected and having to remain in the deliberation room. She wanted to get back to her salon to do business with appointed customers. She said she was losing a lot of money while serving on the jury. She seemed flippant about the charges being levied against the defendant. Someone asked where she worked, but I didn't know the place; I figured it was a popular place where a skilled, hard-working lady could make good money. She was salon groomed with nice hair and make-up, and wore high heel shoes and tight denim pants. She was the type of woman I always tried to stay away from. She spelled trouble to me. I called her, "Trouble." She voted "guilty" several times during our deliberation process and didn't seem willing to change her mind; she just wanted to get out of the deliberating room, get back to work and to hell with a man's future. She seemed indifferent about any man's future.

An older lady sat in the third chair as I moved attention around the table. She told us earlier, before anyone was selected, that she was a farmer's wife and her husband was hard at work out in the fields doing spring planting. I called her, "Farmer's Wife." I knew no one's real name so I continued inventing names to identify them; all remaining fairly anonymous. She was over-weight, had a couple of darkened front teeth and wore a colorful summer dress. She voted "guilty" several times and also appeared to have no desire to change her vote. I had little confidence in her deductive and inductive reasoning ability. I suspected things were simple in her life and she had little to do with the family business. I shouldn't have come to any conclusions concerning her, for all I knew she was brilliant and just didn't want to share.

I didn't want to share either, but did a couple of times to make a point, and was willing even more to sway an opinion. Her weight and bad teeth made her unattractive and there she sat next to pretty, Trouble, all fixed up and ready to hit the streets. I shouldn't have been hard on Trouble either, it's just that I had experienced that kind of woman before, and she seemed troublesome. Farmer's Wife smiled once in a while before being chosen and told a couple of short stories about farming, but later had little to say. Maybe she was being more serious or maybe she was a bit overwhelmed with the process. I was a little puzzled by the whole process myself. Whatever the reason for her quietness, I didn't trust her ability to gather facts, formulate ideas and come up with a verdict without reasonable doubt. I was not sure she wanted to put in the effort.

The next person sat between me and Farmer's Wife was an older man. I caught myself thinking of him as old man several times and described him later to my wife as an old man, but he was a year younger than me. Many people have said I don't look my age and I tend to agree with them. The old man was about five feet nine inches with an average build. He said he had been a lineman before retiring. "In the NFL," I joked. He smiled and said, "No, Public Service, the local electric company. I climbed electrical poles for thirty years."

We had discussed all this before being chosen for the jury and had occasionally joked about him being a lineman. He joked that he had lost a lot of size since his NFL days and commented about losing his size except his belly. He had a nice sense of humor. We could probably have been friends after the trial, but I didn't even ask his name. I named him "Old Man."

I was wary about Old Man at first because I didn't know how he would vote and we might be on opposite sides of the issue. He remained laid-back and light hearted during most of the deliberating, but got annoyed with one of the other jurors. He even got loud once, then whispered to me, "I put up with that kind of shit for thirty years and I'm not going to put up with it from that woman."

He kept voting innocent. He concurred with my cohort, First Lady, at the other end of the table. He listened with an open mind; I, however, figured he wouldn't change his mind.

He loudly said to the foreperson directly across from him that he thought the police were engaged in entrapment; illustrating his point with the idea of a cop sitting behind a billboard with a radar gun. He was quite vehement about the whole thing, appearing to be venting about a negative experience. I tended to believe also that the police were engaged in entrapment, but didn't agree so much about the speeding thing. It was First Lady, Old Man and me who were defending a believed to be innocent man sitting somewhere outside the deliberating room waiting for our decision.

I bet that was a hard place to be, waiting on twelve people to determine his future. I prayed right then and there to never put myself in that kind of situation. I had been very lucky my whole life, having gotten several breaks and reprieves. I had been judged guilty for small offenses and paid the price several times. I had been stupid like the man being judged, but not punished unfairly or harshly for stupidity. I thought it was time for the defendant to get a break. I was there to see that he was judged fairly. I took my responsibility seriously.

Then there was me sitting in the fifth positioned chair. I was the fifth juror originally chosen of the first thirteen and then ironically I found the fifth position chair around the deliberating table. I was actually juror number two in the jury box. I couldn't remember who sat where in the jury box because I didn't make eye contact with hardly anyone except the judge when instructing from his bench and the lawyers when addressing us at the podium. I kept my head down when entering and leaving the jury box. I didn't want anyone to even suspect my feelings or opinions outside the deliberating room. My feelings, however, got known for sure several times by the foreperson. I told her she was disrespectful to me and I didn't appreciate it. She apologized. She asked me another time if I had daughters of my own, saying she had three daughters, and got all emotional about wanting to protect them. I strongly told her that I had two daughters and two granddaughters myself and asked for her to not direct accusations or comments questioning my feelings towards protecting children. I was with Old Man, not going to put up with shit from that woman.

I came into the deliberating room swaying to one side, yet attempting to keep an open mind, feeling all along that the prosecution didn't make a strong case. The lawyer for the prosecution said, and the defense lawyer reiterated, that the prosecution had to make a powerful case against the defendant. I believed they did not make a strong case and that they had not presented enough evidence of guilt, in fact, very little evidence of guilt. I voted innocent on both charges several times because of much doubt of guilt, and couldn't change my mind unless someone presented more evidence or greater reasoning of guilt. I found myself fighting for a man's life, not knowing the consequences if found guilty and afraid, whatever the consequences, that his life would be ruined. I stood strong with First Lady and Old Man.

Next to me at my left in chair number six was the alternate who could not speak or vote, but had to listen to everything and act as if she were one of the twelve chosen jurors in case something happened and one of us couldn't continue. She said she worked at Aldo's in the small town of Delphi; Aldo's being a store kind of like Dollar General. I had never heard of or been in an Aldo's store. I guessed she was about twenty-five years old, probably started working at Aldo's right out of high school. She indicated that Aldo's employed about thirteen people; I guessed she was middle management. I got the feeling she had things to say, but couldn't express her opinions because of being the alternate. I had no idea what she was thinking or how she might vote if given the chance. I called her "Aldo." I suspected Aldo would have little to do with the deliberating process, thinking no one was going to leave the deliberation room that day or any day if more time was needed.

The seventh chair at the end of the table was occupied by a lady I guessed to be around sixty years of age. She kind of served as an anchor for the next two women sitting in chairs eight and nine. She wore extremely thick glasses that made her eyes look huge. I named her "Librarian" because she looked and acted like a librarian, but of course I knew nothing about her; knowing only that she nominated the lady who became the foreperson, saying she had talked with her earlier and thought she was qualified to be the foreperson. I soon figured out that number nine had been campaigning for the job long before anyone else had a chance to think about whom to choose as foreperson. Librarian voted guilty each time and seemed rather set in her opinions, going along with eight and nine chair people on about every position. She seemed nice and appeared to not have bias or hidden motives for believing the defendant was guilty. She questioned some wording of the printed law given to us by the judge. He gave the stapled papers to help guide us through the nuances of a particular section of the law pertaining to this particular trial. The specific law was complicated and seemed to cover any pertinent situation; it seemed up to us to figure out those nuances pertaining to our particular trial. I trusted Librarian to do the right thing in the final analysis. She had an eye for words and their usage. I appreciated her, and thought she was fairly smart and eager to help the jury with words, wording and definitions.

The lady sitting in the eighth chair looked similar to Librarian, but possessed a completely different personality and attitude. She was older with white hair and possessed a stern demeanor. I sensed she was the type of woman who would have taken me to the woodshed as a disobedient child or even presently for that matter. I named her "Woodshed" and was not going to let her get her hands on me or put words in my mind. I also sensed that she didn't like me or Old Man.

She seemed angry and willing to jump to false conclusions, once calling the defendant a pedophile without evidence or reason. I corrected her on that point. I said, "You don't know this man. You don't know if he has a prior record of child molestation. You cannot call him a pedophile without some evidence." She admitted to being wrong and that I was correct. I didn't know from where her anger came, but hoped it wouldn't rub off. Woodshed had voted consistently guilty. I suspected she was not a pleasant person to be around and with whom to associate or debate philosophy. To tell the truth I just didn't like her. I thought she was set in her ways and opinionated. I believed Woodshed was set with her "no" vote.

We were all thinking and reasoning from experience, especially those of us who were older; thinking some people not selected for the jury were dismissed because of lack of age and or experience.

The next lady was the foreperson who accepted the job immediately after being nominated and before any other person could be mentioned. Like I said, she flipped open her notepad, brought out her pencil and began to scribble information before we had a chance to think or speak. She was a large woman, forty pounds over-weight at least and wore her hair in a fake Dorothy Hamill pixy-cut that was died black and framed her very white face. She joyously started the process of being foreperson and deliberation queen without objection, soon asking, "Do you want to take a vote."

No one objected after a brief round table comment session; all were somewhat in the dark about the process of deliberating a criminal case, including picking a foreperson, and how and when to take a vote.

I called the foreperson, "Pixy Face." She had immediately raised her hand and asked, "How many people think he's guilty?" She had done this before anyone had a chance to object.

Her attitude never changed from that point onward. I figured Pixy Face would vote last, but no, she set the tone right away by blurting-out a loud, resounding "guilty," and then went around the table from her left taking our first vote. She appeared to be initially disappointed in three of us, First Lady, Old man and myself for voting innocent. Things got a little ugly from that awkward beginning, in fact things soon got really ugly. Pixy Face got emotional several times, kept going over the same three emails and got disrespectful towards me and First Lady several times. First Lady frequently challenged Pixy Face. I thought Pixy Face had possible issues about men, sex and/ or child molestation. I wished to know her story, but I didn't even know her name. In fact, I never learned anyone's name or even their background.

A few of us shared if we thought it necessary to make a point. I learned only bits and pieces of shared personal knowledge from other jurors. We discussed the fact that our personal experiences had a bearing on our opinions and beliefs, and ultimately our vote concerning guilt or innocence; the law seemed to give leeway for that kind of influence on decision making. We discussed how our personal experiences might influence our final decision.

Someone suggested at one point in our deliberation that maybe a new foreperson should be chosen. Pixy Face said begrudgingly that she would give up the job if someone else wanted it, but no one wanted the job after she had screwed it up so much. Well, anyway, that was how I felt about it. I certainly didn't like Woodshed, but I disliked Pixy Face even more, thinking she had huge biases. I didn't mind her employing experience, that was to be expected, but I was afraid her unpleasant experiences caused hostile bias. I didn't feel sorry for her at that time and place, and couldn't let her negative experiences sway the jury. When someone again expressed the possibility of another foreperson, Pixy Face went on about her business as if no one entertained the idea. She commanded the situation with size, skill and aggressiveness. I agreed again with Old Man about not taking shit from her.

The person in chair number ten was an eighteen year old lady who admitted that she had little experience. She did not say what she did or where she worked, but I suspected she was a student at Purdue. I named her "Purdue." She had little to say except she lacked experience and was young, but felt she yet had opinions and good judgment. I believed she was sincere and would in the final analysis make a conscientious decision without a reasonable doubt. She was nice, and sort of average about everything including looks, size and intelligence. I honestly paid little attention to her during most of the deliberating process because she had little to say. I, however, did understand that her vote carried just as much weight as anyone's vote. I respected Purdue's influential position and important part of the jury.

I had no idea why the lawyers chose her to be on the jury, but then I didn't know the why about anyone sitting at the table, including myself. I did know for some reason that there were three men and ten women chosen for the jury. The three men were older and five of the women were older. The other women tended to be younger. Those numbers probably meant nothing. Purdue was at one end and Librarian at the other end of the women age spectrum. It was almost a Bell Curve when considering the distribution of age. I was the oldest of the men.

The lady sitting in the number eleven chair was about thirty-five, relatively attractive and seemingly very sound of mind and body. She first voted guilty, but began to change her mind while helping us interpret the law. She had a grasp of the ambiguous part of the law that the judge had printed out for us to apply to the case. The law seemed rather complicated and full of ambiguities or ways out of a definite position. She pointed out several words and sort of defined them for our interpretation. I thought she would have made a great foreperson, not because she finally came over to my way of thinking, but because she helped us reason our position. I called her, "Arbiter" for she applied common sense when a few of us were getting emotional and passionate, and needed a little help concerning the final outcome. I wished I had known something about Arbiter before voting for Pixy Face for foreperson. I would have voted for Arbiter.

First Lady was smart and articulate, but she also was a bit emotional and maybe biased. I identified with her even though I thought like Arbiter. Arbiter was definitely the one in retrospect that should have been the foreperson. It was strange how she remained silent until we really needed her. She managed to guide us without known opinion and when the near final vote was taken, I was surprised when she voted "no" concerning guilt. Arbiter had changed her own mind by her own discovery of truth through interpretation of the law. Arbiter probably weighed no more than a hundred and thirty pounds, probably didn't have a college degree and was not aggressive, yet she commanded the last hour or so of our deliberation. She was a true leader and Pixy Face knew it by the time that second day was completed. I saw resignation on that pixy face. I never looked into her eyes after the last vote.

Number twelve person sat opposite First Lady. He was a large fat man who seemed to have few opinions, but finally let his feelings about people who broke the law abundantly clear. He stated several stupid and false facts about criminal behavior that influenced no one. He was probably eighty pounds over-weight and sweaty, and had a hard time getting in out of the jury box. It was a tight fit for me. He wasn't a handsome man. I called him, "Big Guy." He was lucky to be at the near end of the jury box where he could get in and out without waddling past six chairs closely fastened to the floor. The chairs rocked and swiveled, but didn't move from their secured position. Big Guy had no problems in the deliberation room because forty-seven people had fit in that room earlier so there was plenty of walking space. He had little to say and didn't sway anyone's opinion concerning the final vote when he did speak. I noticed Big Guy ate several sandwiches at lunch and sucked down two sodas. I thought Big Guy needed some desert; maybe we both needed some of those crinkle cookies or a piece of blueberry pie my wife makes so well. If I didn't swim three days a week and workout between swim days, I would be heavy like Big Guy. I yet think I'm athletic at the age of seventy-three. I didn't name myself, but if I did of course, it would have been "Handsome." I suspected Woodshed and Pixy Face had a few other names for me and First Lady. I also suspected they would not be flattering names.

The thirteenth person around the table was a small lady I suspected was from India. She could not make up her mind about anything, voting "undecided" every time. She spoke limited English, mostly saying she was undecided. I respectfully named her, "Undecided." She had a quiet, soft voice and a humble appearance. I vaguely heard her from the other end of the table speak to First Lady about being in the deliberation room was much better than housekeeping. Her undecidedness in the final analysis served as a "no" vote concerning guilty.

# May 21, 2014 – 9:45

We continued to pore over the small amount of evidence. Pixy Face kept going over three emails she believed proved the defendant guilty. First Lady kept arguing that the emails were not enough to find the man guilty. I agreed with First Lady and clearly stated my point of view. The same pattern of argument continued until we took another vote with five of us thinking there was considerable doubt. Pixy Face was now beginning to get aggressive towards having her way and find the defendant guilty. She got disrespectful to me and First Lady. I called her out again for being disrespectful to me and she begrudgingly apologized, but never apologized to First Lady.

The bailiff asked if she could get lunch for us and we soon had a variety of sub-way sandwiches and drinks. We nearly ate silently, but I could feel noisy minds working. I had only a small sandwich and drank a little bit of water. I stood near First Lady for a minute or two while getting my sandwich. I whispered to her, "We have to stand by our convictions." She replied, "Yes, we do."

Pixy Face took another vote on both charges and came up with six to six on both counts. Old Man got loud and irritated again with Pixy Face; she, however, had an ally at her right side that kept arguing for guilty. First Lady finally said to Pixy Face, "You can read those emails twenty more times, but that won't give them anymore weight." I agreed with her. We made eye contact and I knew we were cohorts. We had similar convictions and opinions about the two ladies sitting across from me.

Librarian kept voting guilty, but said she was being swayed by the word intent and was not sure if the defendant actually had intent to solicit sex from a fourteen year old child. "There," I declared, "Is the crux of the case. Did he believe she was fourteen? I don't think he ever believed she was fourteen." Several around the table agreed with me.

Pixy Face while in a huff read off the three emails again. "Here he says the younger the better." I replied, "What is younger for a forty-seven year old man. Forty-seven is young to me. Besides he was on a web site for people eighteen and older." The defendant had said that several times during the DVD interview conducted by the police officer.

Maybe we should see the DVD again someone suggested. We all agreed that was a good idea. Pixy Face wrote a note to the judge requesting that we see the DVD again. The Judge gave the bailiff permission to bring us back into the courtroom to again watch the interview. We waited a while, and soon were lining up, passing the two lawyer tables and stepping into the jury box. Everyone watched the whole interview again, judge, lawyers and jurors. I was even more convinced that the defense should have shown the DVD rather than the prosecution. The man seemed human, honest and congenial.

Two people changed their vote after watching the DVD again. Librarian unexpectedly voted innocent. Pixy Face was beyond herself after the vote was taken. It was seven for innocent, one undecided and four guilty. Someone asked Undecided, "So you have doubts?" "Yes, for sure," she replied. I mentally reminded myself about reasonable doubt and vaguely saw Thomas Jefferson sitting in a near corner of the room, nodding approval.

We took a vote on the second charge and it came out six to six again. It appeared we were stuck and that no one seemed willing to budge on their vote. "Shall we tell the judge we are hung?" Pixy Face asked. I suggested we go forward for a little longer and most agreed. We did go about fifteen minutes longer, took another vote, but nothing had changed. I asked Woodshed and Pixy Face if they had any doubt about guilt. They said they had no doubt that he was guilty.

# May 21, 2014 – 3:30

I thought when Librarian changed her vote, Pixy Face would see that she was not going to have her way despite her aggressiveness and rude assertions for guilty. She didn't have her way that day at that time and place. She didn't intimidate anyone in that room; in fact she lost respect from those who originally took her point of view that a few emails proved guilt. It seemed very possible that the defendant never really believed the supposed girl on the other end of the communication was fourteen.

Arbiter changed her mind about the outcome by reading the law, pointing out facts and building a case for an innocent outcome. First Lady and I kept seeing the big picture while Pixy Face saw only a few emails. I kept saying that I could not ruin a man's life for being stupid and careless with his desires. He found someone who was promising all the fantasies imaginable and willing to fulfill them. Little did he know it was some over-zealous police officer with several years of training with whom he was communicating. The police officer knew just what to say and promise to set him up for disaster. It just didn't seem fair to a man who was simply acting with the wrong anatomy part.

Undecided's interpreted "no" vote in the final analysis had real meaning. In the end we all basically voted like Undecided. It was like none of our votes counted one way or another. It was like a tie ball game where there's no winner or loser. It seemed like a waste of time.

I, however, felt the weight of my vote that literally saved a man's life was heavy. There was no winner or loser, but if there was a winner it was the defendant. He was out time and money, sorrow and fear, emotional distress and misery. A mistrial was second best, but "Not Guilty" would have been the best for the defendant. I'm sure a mistrial was not a win for him, yet it was at least temporary relief. I hoped he would escape judgment again, only time would tell. I felt good about my personal decision to vote him innocent. The residual weight of jury duty was over for me, but the defendant might have to go through another weighty trial. I yet felt proud to have served Tippecanoe County.

I mentally saw the deliberation table long after leaving the deliberation room. I saw the thirteen jurors and remembered their pretend names and their final vote.

First Lady – Innocent
Trouble – Innocent
Farmer's Wife – Guilty
Old Man – Innocent
Phillip – Innocent
Aldo – No Vote
Librarian – Innocent
Woodshed – Guilty
Pixy Face – Guilty
Purdue – Innocent
Arbiter – Innocent
Big Guy – Guilty
Undecided - Unsure

So, the initial vote on the solicitation of sex charge was eight jurors voting guilty, three jurors voting innocent and one juror voting unsure. The final vote was four jurors voting guilty, seven jurors voting innocent and one juror voting unsure. Aldo admitted later that she would have voted innocent. The final vote on the charge of solicitation of pornography was six to six.

# New Songs

Ocean sang a
fretted song to
broken spirits.
Pieces of violated
bodies labored
without reward as
they then walked
foreign roads and
toiled mean fields
seeking earth's
fulfilling depth.
Slavery sat apart
reality from
fiction with only
memories of a
homeland.
Deprivation and
lost rights sought
self-invented
new residence.
Human craving
caused created
blue songs of
broken spirits
no orchestra
could duplicate
in abiding humility.
Some saw no
wrong with lack
of empathy as
rhythmic life
labored towards a
blue crossroads.

# Self Help

Courage is
found in a
lonely place
where few
stopover for
human rights.
Good time and
freedom is
tough to find
in that place.
Self valor is
born there to
fill cracks and
crevasses elites
leave alone.
Brave travelers
venture there
into mind
with heaven's
blessing.
Souls contain
white moments
spent there as
black gained
experiences
become gray
conquered trials
Most seek a
calm place to
live in peace,
protected by
one braver
than self.

# Pursuing Freedom

Freedom
in God's
creation is a
purposeful
pursuit.
Its seeds lie
in waiting,
like kindling
expecting
ignition.
It's passion
germinates
no matter
how long
it takes to
accumulate.

A few people
come and
go through life
spontaneously
while most
struggle to
find freedom.

And in
natural pursuit
of freedom,
purpose is
not always
immediately
self-resolved
for seeds are
never lost,
but only lay

waiting for
favorable
conditions to
sprout.

Humans
ever seek
freedom,
no matter
how long
it takes
to coalesce.

People never
come and
go in life with
graceful ease,
but awkwardly
struggle to
gain and keep
their God
given desire
for freedom.

# A Flower's Beauty

A flower's beauty is gauged by
time, effort and final outcome.

> We're born little,
> sculpt life and
> die irrelevant as
> death destroys;
> born crying and
> die whimpering,
> freedom wanting,
> time praying.

> We begin dazed,
> end astonished,
> middle suffering;
> conclude life
> silently alone,
> hopeful of being
> led to heaven
> by an angel.

> We live clothed,
> covering form as
> time shreds and
> body erodes;
> pride dissolves,
> humility solidifies,
> life declines in a
> downward spiral.

A flower's beauty is gauged by
time, effort and final outcome.

# Grasping

I caused change with
one naive action,
chanced losing that
struggled to possess
within my closed fist.
I relaxed my grasp,
glimpsed inside and
saw exposed skin.

I soon realized
God's work clearly
by understanding
amazing anatomy.
I imagined bones,
tendons, nerves,
muscles, veins,
arteries and blood.

Oh, I whispered,
"This in one hand,"
then considered
whole body that
favored openness,
rejected fists and
led me towards a
bit of spirituality.

# Principles Fulcrum

Morality teeters
on a principles
fulcrum where
all consequences
matter within a
liberated society
that cannot wash
passive hands of
responsibility.

Weak ethics
brand slave
owning as fair,
important and
advantageous,
but morality
firmly corrects
humanity's
fulcrum balance.

Weighty control
sways destiny by
counterbalancing
human nature that
sooner or later
detects freedom
amid hostility,
negotiation and
understanding.

# On Ocean's Edge

Waves
that begin
as distant,
British
ocean surges
become
rebelling swells
advancing
destiny;
liberating,
roaring,
generating
courage,
like an aquatic
orchestra
seeking a
magnificent
crescendo;
they soothe
looming
deceptive
danger,
wishing to
find new
liberty,
merging as
revolutionary
thunder.

# Seeking Fairness

Big doesn't
mean
bad and
small doesn't
mean weak.

A gentle
man wishes
peace and
evades
animosity.

A humble
man wields
power and
position for
equality.

A quiet,
reserved
man wishes
fairness and
liberty.

Big builds
free today
while small
pursues
tomorrow.

# Principle

I see
myself as a
useful principle,
coming from a
distant nowhere,
from another
mind state,
nearly another
philosophy.
I live with
increasing
strength and
expression, and
cannot stop at
some line or
intact border.
I disappear
repeatedly,
expounding
morality and
justice, but
then retreat
into obliging
humanity.
I feel moral, but
man's nature
causes me to
doubt myself.
I seem distant,
but I am close
in a natural man's
heart, mind and
soul.

# Moans and Groans

Framers
collectively
grappled,
groaned and
growled until
democratic
answers united.
They jointly
merged
elevations into
foothills to
form a Republic
mountain.

Their assuring
words and
declarations
came with
monumental
shudder and
shaking.
People
understood
Bill of
Rights and
Constitution
significance.

# Songs of Yesterday

A silly melody
that affected
me frequently,
lingered as a
planted song,
cultivated
growing ideas.

I wished it
to be like a
gentle wind,
that caused
my salvation,
on a hot day
in light attire.

I felt secure
when hearing
that song,
victory lauded
freedom,
my spirituality
got altered.

# Sailing by Consent

One who rows a
boat cannot himself
be a boat, yet
both must follow
natural water
flowing basics.
One must
manipulate a
boat with natural
water consent and
even though a
boat builder
creates a sail boat,
sailing is from
consenting wind.

Rivers and
oceans maintain
natural physics,
but a Republic
needs a sailor
who understands
political physics
to justly navigate.
A leader, like a
good sailor, must
understand both
natural wind and
water behavior in
order to acquire
public consent.

# I Close My Mind

I willfully close
my mind to reality,
think economics
instead of liberty,
ignore deviant
principles that
deteriorate truth.
I see black men as
property because
I perceive them
as property,
see them not
as a men, but
something
like a donkey,
cow or horse.
I am blind to
self-governing
principles for all.
I deceive myself
about slavery, and
men owning and
governing others.

Founders
believed that
one man cannot
govern another,
some did and
yet felt it wrong.
No one should
think black men
are not human.

So, I close
my mind to
reality and
open it to
economics.
I fear I'm
destroying
American
government
principles and
sadly ignoring
Declaration of
Independence
and Constitution.
I'm a foolish,
selfish man
seeking war
between states
with ignorance
in heart.
I'm helpless
to see and hear
signs of war,
yet feel it in
my bones, but
am intuitively
preparing for it.

Divided minds
like country
shall soon be.
I fear many
citizen will die
because of
foolish and
selfish people
like me.

# Moan and Speak

I shudder
in disbelief
when long last
answers surface.
I hear men speak
in tearful disbelief
of sovereignty and
self-governance.

I seek retorts
silently waiting
for rivers and
mountains to
speak boldly,
whispers and
significant groans
declare truth.

I hear articulate
answers seeping
and somehow,
someway I learn
own insignificance,
thus intuitively and
spiritually learn
own significance.

o

Righteous men
believe that all
human beings
have rights,
citizenship and
are equal to other

human beings
in society.

Responsibility for
acceptance of
natural rights
falls upon each
human being and a
Republic willing
to accord freedom
for all its citizens.

God bestows
freedom, and
like a mountain
groans truth, and
like a river,
speaks spirituality as
humanity craves
individual freedom.

# Consent

Without
self-discipline
there can be no
self-governing and
without sovereignty
there can be no
true freedom.

Freedom to
govern self is a
magnificent
privilege, and a
consequential
obligation and
undertaking.

Only by consent
can one man
govern another for
in strength of
"We The People"
comes individual
liberty for all.

A Republic is a
representative
government that
allows an elected
few to govern
consenting many
clarifying voters.

# Familiar Song

Passion was
found
when honest
words
spewed from
rebellious
mouths,
debating
guaranteed
rights, for
truth wore a
protective
constitutional
robe while
beating a
freedom drum
to a ravenous
republican
song.

# Re-grain

Debate is home,
enlightenment waiting,
wishing for thousands
to preserve wisdom.

Time always pushes
upward seeking light as
germination struggles
to re-grain life again.

Slender stalks seek
nurtured liberation and
into sun they sprout
from purposeful seeds.

Onward, onward
they push until precious
liberty is re-grained to
embellish mature life.

Onward, onward
liberated stalks ascend,
first one then hundred,
then a noticed million.

Time forgets those
consumed, lost and
re-grained as history
repeats sought destiny.

# Liberated Vessel

It was oddly shaped
like wood on a lathe,
forcefully held,
fastened and contained,
thrown into rotation.

In awkward creation,
revolving and evolving,
tools in graceful hands
shaped and polished an
emancipating vessel.

Some saw a crude,
simple entity while
others saw political art
uniquely designed with
thoughtful creativity.

It was organic material
carefully hand crafted,
skillfully turned and
lovingly contrived with
spiritual hands.

Founders imbibe,
tasted liberty with it,
for in unique debate a
judicial container was
artfully shaped.

# My Precious Hand

In my closed
Hand lies
God's essence for
He made
My hand,
Taught it how to
Clasp and
Move with
Significance.
I possess precious
Hand gifts, and
Faith enough to
Capture intangible
Possibilities.
I yet fear
It might wane and
I would be
Sorrowfully left
With only
Hand memories.
I scribe
Providential
Words with
My hand.
Power between
Hand and
Pen make
Me pray for
Divine guidance
With two
Clasped hands

# Closed

Within closed
wary hand,
I cannot find
strength as
mind is
closed to peace.
Perhaps I hold
too tightly or
cloister too well.
I study
closed hand,
see form and
function and
realize that
I create a fist
while grasping.
Do others
see a fist and
suspect
aggression?
I open
fist and
mind, and find
security and
sincerity.
I give amity
to another
who needs
it greatly
while clasping
their hand
in friendship.

# Hungry Time

On earth time cruises.
Minds celebrate existence.
Day's light engages earth.
Spiritual realm seeps humanity.
Wheat's golden color arrives.
Time is just in time.
Night expects sun's brilliance.
Stalks surrender to thrashing.
Grain is ground and punished.
Stomachs recognize hunger.
Bread also feeds mind.
Spirits seek thoughtful time.
Tomorrow waits celebration.
Time bakes every day.
Bread is also for tomorrow.
Hungry stomachs speak.
Full mouths are silent.
Bread has no enemy.
Bribery is cheap.
Liberty is expensive.
Spirits know conspiracies.
Time is magnificent.
Minds ignorantly celebrate.
Freedom doesn't relinquish cheaply.

# Chapter VIII

# Burden of Proof

# May 21, 2014 – 4:30

The burden of proof was in the hands of the prosecution while the defense had to prove nothing—the prosecution failed to prove their case—I knew it right away and others followed three of us into a doubtful area through reasoning. I felt good because I literally helped save a man's life, at least for a while. His future was unlike the solid oak table behind which he boldly sat.

First Lady, Old Man and I worked to build a case for presumed innocence beyond a reasonable doubt. I think other's voted their conscience and that was remarkable. The system worked even though we came up with no verdict. I kept wondering what the defendant was thinking after learning our outcome; was he happy or sad, relieved or anxious, calm or angry. I recall again our final vote that came down to four people holding out for guilty while seven of us voted for innocent and of course there was Undecided who actually made the count eight to four.

First Lady – Innocent
Trouble – Innocent
Farmer's Wife – Guilty
Old Man – Innocent
Phillip – Innocent
Aldo – No Vote Alternate
Librarian – Innocent
Woodshed – Guilty
Pixy Face – Guilty
Purdue – Innocent
Arbiter – Innocent
Big Guy – Guilty
Undecided - Unsure

I caught a glimpse of the old metal elevator often while sitting in the jury box. It momentarily distracted me. We were kind of like that elevator for a while, up and down, up and down. I, however, was confident that we had done the right thing by insisting on more evidence, more proof. Some of us were like that old modernized elevator; willing to change, but begrudgingly open yet wary of change. Some of us were resilient and unwilling to give up our identity. Some of us were like that elevator, willing to carry others to the top and bottom of the decision making process. Two of us especially carried the weight of a man's life on our shoulders. We were Otis elevators for a short time in the deliberating room.

Freedom prevailed at many levels during my two days in Superior Court One. It all began with filling out a questionnaire. Freedom blossomed when I drove downtown, walked into the courthouse, got selected for duty, listened to two lawyers argue for and against a man's future and finally deliberated a man's freedom.

I love that word "freedom," love this United States of America, and love our system of government. Freedom speaks to me when I see the American flag. Freedom thoughts sometimes make me tear up for those who have sacrificed a little like me or a lot like others.

I find new beauty on every travel trip to explore America, but every time I see that red, white and blue stars and stripes, I get melancholy.

I served in the military so maybe I have a special respect for the flag. I get a little choked-up when thinking about all those who have died for this country, our way of life and our freedom.

I concluded especially after serving two days in Superior Court One that the majority of people in this country feel as I do and have a natural need for life, liberty and the pursuit of happiness. I concluded that the majority of people wish to rule themselves rather than be ruled and that power should come from the bottom up and not the top down. I sometimes question how true the desire or maybe the knowledge of "self-rule" is in many parts of the world.

People are our Republic in the final analysis. Average people serve this country every day and continue to save our precious experiment one life at a time.

# Intelligence

I use power when
others will not
reason by lack of
inherent nature

I use violence
when others by
unwarranted
convictions
will not bargain
cooperate or
compromise.

My duty is to
God and thus
humanity for
I am a free,
unique person
seeking peaceful
resolution.

Intellectual
ethics guide
my mind and
hand to write
opinions,
laws and
documents.

My sword to
defeat enemies
is guided by
righteousness.

# A Core

Is a human a person
without a spirit or a
Republic a nation
without humanity?

So little life is
in tree bark,
apple peel or
human skin,
thus a shell is
superficial and
not an essence
quantity.
A declaration
is a beginning
measure for
revolution.
A formal
Declaration of
Independence is
bark, shell,
peel and skin for
inner legislative
Constitution,
Bill of Rights and
Republic core.

Is a human a person
without a spirit or a
Republic a nation
without humanity?

# Liberated Ocean

Ideas and
philosophies
came far in
time and
space as a
few men
labored
fiercely to
express
thoughts,
adapt
ideas and
perpetuate a
philosophy.

Courage
rose in
time and
space as
Founders
drank sweet
liberating
milk, and
created a
Constitution
establishing
rule from a
mother's
breast.

It was
fifty-six
poised men
beating and
shaping rocks,

smoothing and
forming sand,
making a
novel shore
to mature
colonies into
states with
intervals and
weightiness.

They bravely
justified
means and
presented a
magnificent
document,
churned milk
into butter
on a liberating
shore of an
ocean crossed
by ancestors
to establish a
Republic.

# Direction of a Union

America's
beginning, like
bison seeking
grass and water,
gave unfamiliar
definitions as
Founders
sought hope in
time's rigid,
toughness with
philosophy.

They sensed
greatness and
awareness,
felt new earth
beneath feet and
crossed rivers
to embrace and
established an
alliance to
journey a
fanatical path.

# Re-souled

One itinerant
philosophy
was brought
to live again,
be re-souled;
a republican
freedom seed
got chosen
like wheat;
a republican
idea got
placed safely,
watched over
until right time
to germinate
in new soil.

It was not
luck that
brought this
idea to
stalk and
grain again;
Founders
brought one
principle to
one state,
then to
ten states,
then to
thirteen states.

Blessed
civil grain
produced a
Republic that
grew and
became a
potent entity.

Ancestors
possessed
brilliance
to choose a
Republic;
they indeed
were civil wheat
producers,
aspirating
freedom lovers
strong enough
to establish a
new Republic
on a new
continent with a
new democratic
philosophy.

# Discovering

Finding seed
present within
is discovering
pure essence,
like finding
apples in a
silver bowl.

Finding spirit
in earthly
humans is
like wise men
finding piety in
own silver soul.

Through
self-awareness,
each finds
wisdom where
God sleeps
in gathering
history.

A golden apple
in a silver frame
resembles a
Declaration of
Independence
framed by a
Constitution.

Liberty is
discovering
one's golden
seed and

silver essence
while justifying
natural laws.

Wisdom
offers images of
hungry men,
self-awareness,
documents and
discovery of
natural laws.

# Broken Mirror

I stare at a
ruthless mirror,
seeing a fast
arriving true
reflection, a
historic image
of gray hair,
lined face and
speckled eyes.
My image is a
book cover for
silently collected
inner memories.
My old face
shrieks like an
often heard
battle cry for
revolution.
Less time gives
more incentive
to think and
remember.
Less time causes
me to feel,
write and sing a
cheerful song.
Oh, mirror
break yourself,
not me, for
I have much
yet to achieve.

# Damn Church Bell

A bell tolls in
distant church
reminding me of
liberty for all.
Its knell serves
me well in time of
unrelenting agony.
I read two
documents again.
They serve well
my purposeful
actions and
resounding
determination.
There passion
yet resounds
eighty-seven
years later.
I wish to hear
only a small
bell calling
me to dinner,
instead of that
damn church bell
tolls death.
My divided
house is crashing.
I must be a
humble carpenter
seeking divine
providence to
rebuild
tomorrow.

# Two Documents

I am a citizen
who whispers
questions, yet
demands to
foster a novel
perfect union.

I studied
Declaration of
Independence and
am beginning
to understand
Constitution.

Oh, these
magnificent
documents give
me hope and
strength to
better life.

I wish to
lift mind
higher and
drive ambition
to a brave
level to act.

My full being
absorbs
liberty as if
thirsty soil
cherishing rain
with no apology.

# One Man

Like a shadow
caused by a
static sundial,
noted history
gets diminished
of control.
Promises are
ignored as
doubt claims a
divided union.
Distress is
coercing liberty
while slavery
is righteously
safeguarded.

Many fear blood
will soon soak
battlefields and
knotted ropes
will follow.
Sweet freedom
grows lonely as
one man stands
between two
passionate ideas
seeking different
outcomes.

# Moral Truth

I am a black
follower, a
moving image
traversing earth.
I change,
enlighten and
make honest an
ignorant society
that ignores
time principles.

I do not hide
evil's face or
alter its truth
of society's
sinful choices.
If absent,
could another
substitute
my accuracy or
exact timing?

I'm a shadow
who alters
with help from
something greater
than self.
Pure sunlight
surely creates
my existence,
for I need a
greater sun.

# Momentary Pause Recognition

Historical time
pauses during
momentary notice,
deciding outcomes
that affect a nation.
These brilliant
moments shape
moral destiny and
honorable behavior.
To recognize
such a moment and
benefit from it,
frequently means
doing nothing.
Our Founders
knew this and
exceptionally
followed
"momentary pause
recognition" by
writing a brief
Constitution that
was a foundation,
not a whole house.

They realized a
wise nation
must pause to
think as time
changes people and
events change a
dynamic country.
Republic
aspects often
change while

human nature
remains static.

Liberty
must grow,
evolve and
mature for a
nation to
flourish,
progress and
authenticate
itself as a free,
exceptional nation.

Change is
guided by
moral truth
that makes
momentary
pausing
recognizable and
brilliant.

Pilgrims were
earth movers,
Founders,
Masons and
all citizens
carpenters
building a
durable,
beautiful house
with patience.

# Magnificent Thoughts

Few people
conjure superb
thoughts that
covertly arise
to encourage
legislative body,
mind and soul.

They come
from history,
philosophy, art
and science like
salty water to
enhance political
nourishment.

Some people
give resolve and
courage while
others arrive
quietly and
humbly with
little notice.

Most grow
overtly like
seeds to flowers,
but some grow
covertly like
magnificent
bloom to fruit.

# Anguish

My natural way is
not your way and
my beliefs are
unlike your beliefs.
I hear a brief
liberty melody
shifting to a
military song.
I hear sweet
flutes and violins
becoming harsh
drums and bugles.
They drift on a
far slung breeze.
I sense most
everything
disjointedly as
I become
lightheaded from
too much wine.
I reminisce
about yesterday,
dream of
tomorrow and
doubtfully speak
about remaining
together as
one nation today.
I'm afraid
reconciliation
is lost in
drum and bugle
reverberation.

# Measuring

Our Republic
did not measure
freedom in
years or English
pounds, but in
time and
determination.

Our Republic
was built by and
for people, and
mostly for
objective and
passionate
self-rule.

Our Republic
corrected true
freedom measures
by naturally
relating to all
people being
created equally.

# Success

Few nations
find true
freedom for
it dwells only
within suffering
spirits of
blessed beings.

It subjectively
embraces
decisions made
intuitively within
subconscious
means to a
liberated end.

It objectively
opens moral
doors of a
great evolving
American
experimental
dream.

Few nations
find true
freedom for
it naturally
lives within a
republic of
"We The People"

# I Fear

My confidence
in our nation
is thirsting for
security,
like willow tree
roots reaching for
needed water.

Hearts and
minds ache as
thirty-four states
reach for solutions,
but eleven
wish cessation.

Security is a myth,
inner courage
hides within
earthen souls.
My thirsty
humanity seeks
desperate
absorption, but
I fear
Jefferson Davis
is leading a
confederation
towards war.

Forgive
my awkward
silence,
obtuse thinking and
hidden plotting.

Forgive
my willow-ness for
I fear,
here in 1861,
Abraham Lincoln
will have to
reach far for
solutions.

I fear
he will have to
reach far for
peace and
security, and
unification and
healing of a nation.

# Security Is a Myth

I bit my lip
yesterday for
naive ideas
nearly escaped
my mind.
My tempted
hands reached
for a pen to
compose a
constitution.

A willow tree
raising water
has adaptablity.

I became an
easygoing tree-
like person,
bending and
reaching for
natural ideas.
Mental roots
reached wildly
claiming ample
thoughts like
covert water.

Logic became
innately mine,
mythical security
disappeared as
I seized fear.

# Awareness of Sanity

War consumes
quickly and fully as
horrible thoughts
promote insanity.
Time slinks towards
tomorrow with no
realized conscience,
threatening to
appropriate sanity.
War provokes foolish
impulses and
transforms once
superb thoughts and
fanciful interludes
into woeful combat.
There are no
brilliant battles,
no mysterious
decisions made, for
planning death and
destruction is
tough to design.
If God would
touch minds
more deliberately,
allow peace in
His infinite realm,
wouldn't sanity
be a planned
consequence?

# Fifty Cannon Balls

North and
South called
it rebellion,
civil disobedience,
insurrection, but
it was known
in final analysis
by one spoken
word, "war."

Lincoln
could call it
whatever wished,
but those
fighting
called it war.
Both sides seemed
to legitimize
the constitution.

Preventing
rebellion and
thus insurrection
vanished with fifty
cannon balls
fired upon
Fort Sumter at
Charleston in
1861.

# Eighty Seven

A hundred and sixty thousand men met as
two armies, and fifty-thousand casualties
never walked Gettysburg fields again.

Abraham Lincoln mournfully spoke for
two minutes four months later, saying
many gave lives so a nation might live.

That damaged United States of America
did live again in liberty and justice, and
dedicated to all men being created equally.

Lincoln reminded that our forefathers
created and dedicated a new liberated
nation just eighty-seven years previously.

# Emancipator

Black skinned
slaves lived
insecurely,
moving like
scared wind
through halls,
then hiding like
darkness behind
closed doors.
A document
that proclaimed
freedom
became a
protective wall
built with
courage.
Many created
biases and
made unfair
decisions, but
one man, a
Commander-
in-Chief,
sought
emancipation.
Strong winds
ceased and
threatened
no more.
A secure nation
matured from
destruction,
death and
sorrow.

# Old Clocks

Featureless
faced clocks
cannot smile or
even frown.
Their unequal
narrow hands are
not hands at all,
but sharp
little swords
that cut and
slash time.
Their hands
cannot reach,
beckon or
draw life close.
Clocks
fear stares,
wish only
glances, for
they shun
truth and
haunt reality.
Clocks lie,
cheat and
threaten, and
seldom make
anyone happy.
They impart
time only with
stoic faces,
risky hands and
annoying little
tick, tick, ticks.

# Chapter IX

# *Hung Jury*

# May 21, 2014 – 5:00

We took a final vote before sending a note to the judge because nothing changed and we were not close to a verdict. Someone asked if this was what you call a "hung jury." Someone else replied, "Yes," end of discussion. It didn't take a rocket scientist to realize that it was impossible for the present twelve people to arrive at a unanimous verdict. After all, there were the foreperson and her cohort sitting next to her, and then there were juror number one and myself who were not going to change our minds. There were those few jurors who did come over to our way of thinking, but little hope for others it seemed. There was no hope for acquittal even if more did decide the man was innocent. There were two domineering, aggressive and myopic women with their heels dug in.

Word came by way of the bailiff that the judge wished us back into the courtroom. We walked down the hall, through the double doors, past the lawyers at their respective tables and stepped into the jury box. I, as usual, did not kept my eyes downward looking at that familiar gray carpet. I had no idea if the other jurors did the same or if they ever avoided eye contact at all.

We remained standing until the judge asked us to be seated. He spoke about what we already knew, seemingly communicating with the lawyers about our inability to come to a unanimous vote. He asked us jointly as a jury if we had anything to say. I blurted without really thinking, "We needed more evidence." Juror number one said, "I don't think we can come to a unanimous decision."

The judge nodded, and then asked the lawyers to join him in the side room, apparently to discuss what to do next. It was the room where certain matters were unrecorded, pertinent matters between only judge and lawyers.

They were not in the room long. The lawyers returned swiftly and remained standing. "You may be seated," the judge clearly gave permission. He explained the circumstances of our indecision to everyone and talked a little bit about the encumbered circumstances of the court.

Abraham Lincoln is regarded as a great hero because of being a leader and having a huge impact on this country during our greatest crisis. He was a remarkable man who came from humble beginnings to become president. He was a man who had to make great decisions and stand-by those decisions against horrible opposition. He was said to be distinctively human and had a pleasing personality. Some say he was the savior of our nation. He eloquently spoke about democracy and that self-government was something all nations should strive to achieve. I thought about my ultimate decision during the trial and imagined Lincoln's weighty decisions. Surely I used the same process of decision making, but not nearly the same consequences. I thought about my responsibility even though I was only deciding the destiny of one man. I, however, felt the responsibility of possibly altering a man's future. Lincoln had a nation to protect.

I am paraphrasing what the judge said, but it was something like: I understand that you the jury cannot come to a consensus, and given the numbers of votes presented to me by the bailiff, I understand why. I will have to declare a mistrial. I want to thank you all for your service and remind you that you don't have to speak to anyone about the case. You, however, can speak to anyone concerning your experience here during these two days in Superior Court One. I would like to speak to you all if you would remain in the deliberation room after we are done here. I am sure the lawyers in this case would also like to speak with you. If you need to leave I understand.

I clearly remember the judge saying, "Thank you again for your service."

# New Degree

I mutely question
quilted night sky,
seek early history,
listen to universe
share wise ideas.

Founders speak,
teach and guide
me towards future
power solutions
for my Republic.

I cleanse mind,
body and soul with
inner philosophy
reflection caused
by moon-lit sky.

Seems God
created water and
sky to speak
naturally with
my mind and soul

I gather flowing
optimistic answers,
understand and
discover reflective
republican tactics.

# Oh, Henry Ford

Oh, look at
Henry and
his immigrant
employees
who speak
no English
while altering
      America,
      industrializing
      automobiles,
      customizing life,
      modernizing
      our exceptional
      country that's
            indeed valid and
            operating in a
            free pulsating
            America that's
            getting livelier
            paint and a
            bigger engine.

# Day Breaking Answer

Many were
hungry and
feared not
living another
penetrating
night.

They endured
mountains and
unending plains.

They set jaw,
gritted teeth,
explored
America.

Days, nights,
months, years
accrued misery,
but joy of a
new life
rewarded
pain and
fear.

Hardship
helped mature
America.

# Mind and Matter

I closed
eyes,
dove in,
thinking
air was
special.
I felt
water's
softness
against
my willing
mind.
I inhaled
surface air,
exhaled
beneath
surface.
I became
one with
environment,
order and
government.
I thought
it wonderful,
swimming
in America.
Did Jefferson
know how
to swim by
nature's rules?
I learned
how to bathe
in freedom's
glory.

# Change

Change is no
sought passion,
but like rain,
it mysteriously
seeks dusty soil
in order to
grow flowers.
Governments, like
rain, sometimes
require dark
thick clouds and a
storm's backside.

Politicians must
embrace change's
strength while
not fearing it, for
change is like a
dynamic storm,
altering life with
gentle touch or
ruthless tempest.

People revel in
stable possibilities,
but in fact,
sweet stability
seldom exists.
Life emerges
through sufficient
accountability in a
free man's eyes.
America is
reverting to
simpler times

when nearly
forgotten
principles were
like rain
seeking dusty soil
to again grow
peaceful flowers.

Americans are
altering and
transforming, but
not abandoning
what has brought an
exceptional nation to
historical heights.
They are allowing
change to manifest
constitutional
processes,
making a more
perfect union
through passionate
change.

# Shifting Sand

Tyrants build
foundations
on shifting
sand and
houses with
dishonest
predictions.

Sailors plot
headings
with historical
compasses and
build boats
with solid
principles.

Creators build
remarkable
boats and
exceptional
liberated
houses with
natural laws.

Americans give
authority with
human nature
qualities and
hopefully build a
solid freedom
foundation.

# Mind Window

Mind windows are
receiving ideas and
promoting solutions
as if cerebral seeds
are wind scattered.

Organic thoughts are
being fashioned,
planted, fertilized and
harvested in soft gray
human mind loam.

This is taking place
while natural laws
intellectually guide
humanity's growth
within time's reward.

Even earthy grit and
persistent seed will
never abandoned
steady human nature
germinating in minds.

Accomplishment is
human nature planting
God's created ideas,
growing and cultivating
them in natural soil.

# My Old Military Hat

Sometimes I feel
my old hat won't fit.
Seems I've had it a
hundred years and
I'm well past two
hundred years old.

Time tore sails,
history died and
old laws waited
for evolution.
Liberty prices are
unnaturally high.

Minds are frayed,
hands can't grip,
mouths struggle
to speak, but
bright stars and
stripes are waving.

We reside in an
altered nation, but
some think America
is mis-sized and
liberty is an old
blue worn out hat.

# Thousands of Years

Some think
history
evolves
in some
natural
progressive
manner
in which
human nature
changes with
passing
time, but
human nature
has not
changed in
two-thousand
years since
Aristotle or
even Christ
for that matter.

# Philosophical Heights

We are polarizing
time travelers,
shaking earth and
uncovering
precious stones.
We seek
mountaintops where
conflicting drama
exists between
real dark truth and
false poetic justice.
We are searchers,
well disguised as
faithful practitioners,
building a special,
better cultivated
spiritual realm.
Only saints on a
wild holiday would
explore such
learned heights.

o

Philosophy
arises in
aftermath of
shared extremes,
like falling
snowflakes
dusting earth
in warm
October sunlight.

o

We are
strewn knowledge
collectors,
walking ancient
worn streets,
discovering ideas
while holding
fellow travelers'
callused hands.
We struggle on
uneven and
rough paths,
searching for a
perfect
philosophy.
We're becoming
intimate realists,
courageously
flirting with truth
on winding paths.

o

Philosophy
arises in
aftermath of
shared extremes,
like falling
snowflakes
dusting earth
in warm
October sunlight.

# Gentle Caress

I slide into
cool soft
seclusion,
warily
seizing a
new scheme.
I then lower
myself into
accepting
welfare that
caresses
mind and
welcomes
false security.
I soon slide
deep into it
past shoulders,
finally over
foolish head.
I shudder a
little from
demeaning
assistance,
but soon
adapt,
feeling one
with it.
I lastly wish
to move
forever in
its gentle
caressing
shame.

# Two Minds

A progressive
mind believes in
changing much
while hiding
behind a curtain.
A republican
mind believes in
speaking well
before a
representative
audience.
A progressive
mind believes in
discovering little
on a dim narrow
catwalk with a
socialistic
philosophy.
A republican
mind believes
in illuminating
reality on an
open stage with
constitutional
principles.

# Separation

Lines separating
red and white
stripes, and
blue and white
stars symbolically
connect and
poetically explain
American history.
Their purposeful
division defines
beginning and
loyal evolution.
Constitutional
joining of
self-rule
truly bonds
freedom for all.
Separation of
colors defines an
American flag like
moments between
day and night,
up and down; and
good and evil
define a nation.
It's long term
group progress and
short term
individual liberty
intermingle
political divisions.

# Arrangement

America senses
like a toddler
knowing little,
speaking little,
thinking little,
suspecting good,
seeking character.

America grasps
obstacles and
opportunities
while learning
to discover
truth and
knowledge.

America joins
three separate
powers like
rivers and
oceans with
liberty and
justice.

America yields
to legislative,
executive and
judicial parts
to comingle
fair laws with
human nature.

# Like a Barn

A Republic is
like an old,
strong hewed,
solid barn with
ethics holding
its many parts
firmly together.

Declared liberty,
Constitution and
Bill of Rights are
like weathered
yet strong beams
fastened together
for a free society.

Our barn is
held together
forever with
constitutionally
driven pegs.

America's
construction
began in 1789,
seemingly a
long time ago
as far as real
Republics exist.

Some folks wish
to underwrite a
slow miserable,
suffering death
to our Republic

out of ignorance
of free principles.

Our barn is
held together
forever with
constitutionally
driven pegs.

Some bang,
sharp talk,
crumble and
irritate to
warp and
alter liberty's
intensity.

Natural laws,
however, and
human nature
will sacrifice all
on American
battle fields to
preserve liberty.

Our barn is
held together
forever with
constitutionally
driven pegs.

# Obtain and Maintain

I travel
my nation with
swelling interest.
Oddly shaped
regions draw
awkward
landscapes that
I labor to map.
State by state
my intrigue
increases with
each personal
surveying tool:
chain, pen and
recording journal.

Contrasts feed
gathering
thoughts and
play with
my psyche
like some
roughness
wanting
smoothing to
gain relevant
attention.
Liberty and
justice
stir pride as
I explore.

I get a
ringing in
my head and a
swelling in
my heart.
I praise,
respect and
love this
United States of
America, as
did our
Pilgrims and
Founders, as
do most
present citizens.

Freedom is
not easy to
obtain,
maintain or
understand for
it surely is
like a forever
changing
survey map
requiring
relentless
pledging of
life,
honor and
wealth.

# Like a Melody

Rights are like a
guitar strumming a
compelling melody
vibrating humanity
naturally as
God provides
immutable energy.

Rights are for
spiritual beings
trapped in
earthy bodies
searching for
own structured
immutable energy.

Rights are like
black and
white energy,
like lighting and
snuffing out
own candle with
immutable energy.

Rights celebrate
seas sailed and
dreamt harmonies
freely plucked
from grace and
own humanly
played melodies.

o

Pilgrims sailed a
philosophical
ocean with beliefs
in toiling against
tyranny with
undaunted faith
in natural forces.

They entered a
cold salty ocean,
wishing to sail
melodic waves of
immature ideas
without fear or
intimidation.

They found
rational rights
within themselves
for humanity had
held them there
long before
setting out to sea.

Found truths and
possessed rights
beyond time seeped
within Pilgrims until
unalienable energy
caused a declaration
of independence.

# Beautiful Freedom

Forty black pearls
silently held as
coerced guests
got dropped.
They scattered
like rain in
liberating reveal,
unlike simple
sand grains,
irritating nature to
create unusual
beauty.

Who with simplicity creates
such perfect and tough beauty
in an oyster's dark dominion?

On bent knees,
someone gathered
beautiful freedom
believers, and
with proclamation
rejoined them as
brothers and sisters.
A natural string
again assimilated
social injustice for
forty beautiful
black neckless pearls.

Who with forgiving time
creates, enslaves and shackles
unjustly such freedom lovers?

# Rusty Nails

Like an old
rusty nail,
freedom principles
hold a nation together.
History brings
wisdom, but
not a nation's soul,
time cannot erode
human rights.

Our nation is
like an old jetty,
rusty nail fastened,
reaching outward,
further than
ever before,
into unfamiliar
cold, salty,
deep waters.

This fastening,
holding and
extension makes
her spirit creak and
awakens a world
waiting for
leadership,
rusty nails and
all.

# Less

Less and
less
I become
an old
eroding
hero statue,
a bit of
sculptured
granite
history
vanishing.
I used
to be
a magnificent
rock piece
giving
inspiration,
but now
I am
a stone
with only
artful
thoughts
remaining,
melting into
sand grains
as God
deems
me time to
to weather
gracefully.

# Two Views

Newton and Darwin
saw worldly light alike,
from a single source
seeking humanity as if
God's hand allowed
creation and evolution.

Every human being is a
creator working with
what God has provided,
with a Godly hand here and
there from time to time,
helping human progress.

To say both are completely
right or wrong is wrong, but
to say both are right is right,
for joining two edifying views
is revelation and reasoning at
work in God caused minds.

# Constructionist

Truth is an
illusion like
everything, a
false perception
made real in
human brains,
minds and
finally souls.
Truth is as
illusionary as
weight of thought,
for no two people
think alike.

All people are
eyewitness at
one time or
another and
no two people
describe scenes,
happenings and
circumstances
identically.
Eyewitnesses are
nearly useless for
relating illusion
is delusional.

There are
billions of
perspectives,
millions of
eye witnesses,
hundreds of
participants, but

only one illusive truth.
Each person is an
eyewitness to a
unique universe,
like a carpenter with
saw and hammer.

A carpenters
fabricates how
he wishes and
perceives things
to be real with
brain, mind and
finally soul.
He practices
reality-illusion-
recognition for
that is his life.
He helps God
evolve things.

Most carpenters,
moment by
moment, and
day by night
believe false fears
after resting and
reasoning with a
little bit of faith,
yet fear is an
illusion that must
be accepted as
aptly relevant
to be defeated.

Reality is an
illusion that
causes each day
to happen.
Choosing to
accept reality and
what it created is
not creating;
but accepting own
perceived truth
is being prudent,
for illusion
is as real as it gets.

o

I silently sit on a
mountain top
day dreaming,
imagining what
might be, finding
myself building
atop what is, for
my mind is the
mountain on which
I noisily contrive
my universe.

# Sixteen Color Thinking

I had sixteen
crayons with
black, white, red,
yellow and brown
skin colors.
Racial prejudice
was simple.
I colored with
distinction and
thought as taught.
Thirty-two colors
got invented, then
sixty-four, and
now crayons are
nearly lost in
colored pencils,
markers, rouge sticks,
paint brushes and
who knows
what else.
My mind contains
hundreds of
colors and
shades as does
my society.
I hardly know
how to be
prejudiced anymore.
Prejudicial shades
are so numerous,
I hardly know
who to call what
names or think of
'as different.

I wish to
return to
sixteen simple
colors, but not
back to ignorant
prejudices.

And, how can
I color
religious prejudice
except in
red blood color?
Peaceful pastel
colors should express
ethnic and religious
differences.
I long for
sixteen simple color
thinking again with
moderate pastels
coloring word,
thought and deed
pictures.
I wish to blend
God's intentions into
moderate human
understanding.
I wish to color
race not black,
white, red,
yellow or brown,
but tolerant.

# Angry Weeds

Open your mind
to a world waiting
liberty restoration.
Take it to a place
where awareness
does not sit silently.
Take it to a place
where hurtful words are
placed in drawers and
lies are lost to a
tolerant liberty quest.

>Teach folks to suppress
>angry weeds and
>liberate calm flowers.

Your awareness
is like a hailstorm
beating down and
denting minds as if
hurtful words and
lies are angry weeds
needing inattention.
Open your mind
to tolerant flowers
that display liberty and
suppress anger.

>Teach folks to suppress
>angry weeds and
>liberate calm flowers.

# Diversity

Build
a fireplace from
dissimilar shape,
size and color
creek rocks,

then compare
it to one built
from same gray
concrete blocks
and red bricks.

Now compare
a country made
of diverse
rather than
homogenous people,

and in this process
of building
you will
surely discover
America.

# Phantom Shadows

A full moon appears,
creating long shadows
that timely dwindle,
then lengthen again,
giving likeness seen
with new perspective.

Strange how parallel
shadows switch their
existence by moon's
power to destroy and
restore truth without
shadow's permission.

Liberating shadows
ever have potential,
present without will,
needing only light to
illustrate exact shape
like truth phantoms.

# Chapter X

# *Forefathers Intent*

# May 21, 2014 – 5:15

I thanked the bailiff for her help and told her she did a great job. I think she liked hearing that because few people probably grasp her importance to the judicial process. She took care of business without really being noticed. I know the judge appreciated her for sure.

I saw the defense attorney while exiting the deliberation room and entering the rotunda of the courthouse. He was standing near the stone railing of the center rotunda going through some papers. I didn't know if he was waiting on someone to talk to or just unwinding. I shook his hand while telling him what a good job he did. The judge had told us in the deliberation room, after the trial, that we had two of the best lawyers in the area in our courtroom. I believed him. I later found out that the prosecution lawyer was chosen to be a federal prosecutor. That said a lot to me about his competency.

The defense lawyer solidified my thinking that I was on the right side of justice. He told me the defendant had served in the military, gone to work every day, paid child support properly, and had only been in trouble with the law one time and that was for drinking twenty-two years ago. He was like a model citizen as far as the lawyer was concerned. I was reassured about the system and how I had operated within it. I was further compelled at that point to think and write about my experience while serving on the jury.

I couldn't help but think about the foreperson and her friend who wanted blood and how close we came to a different outcome. I couldn't help but think about First Lady, Old Man and myself as we kept saying no and stuck to our convictions. What if we had not been there, not been strong and not been resolute? I thought we saved a man's life at that time, in that place and with that courage.

A modern hero of mine was Ronald Reagan who played many roles in life. He was a radio announcer, movie star, union boss, television actor, governor, conservative critic and lecturer, and most importantly, President of the United States. I can yet hear him say, "Mister Gorbachev, tear down this wall." I think he was much like Jefferson, Washington and Lincoln. I think history many times chooses the person to lead. History picks the right person for the right time. Reagan was that person for that time of need. I fear we need another American hero today. I certainly believe that the Founders knew what they were doing when writing the Constitution and the Bill of Rights. They surely had divine guidance. How could that much wisdom be gathered in one place at that time for the formation of an experimental form of government if divine guidance had not been present?

Our Republic surely is a wonderful form of government that protects and assures every one of the right to life, liberty and the pursuit of happiness.

And so goes my liberated mind that is free to think and speak, and judge the rights and responsibilities of others. I am free to write about life, liberty and the pursuit of happiness. I am free to serve on a jury to judge another human being and to decide if a person can continue to have their full rights. I am no American hero, but I am a man who knows his responsibilities and I am free to decipher truth from fiction, guilt from innocence.

Our Republic stands alone in the world as a beacon of hope and a configuration for success. I say don't let anyone falsely speak of equality. Don't let anyone: be they a lawyer, policeman, witness, judge or juror, cause any person to believe less than the truth. A juror can only seek the truth and come to a personal conclusion concerning a person's guilt or innocence.

The preamble of the Constitution reads as follows: "*We the People of the United States, in Order to form a more perfect Union, establish Justice, insure domestic Tranquility, provide for the common defense, promote the general Welfare, and secure the Blessing of Liberty to ourselves and our Posterity, do ordain and establish this Constitution for the United States of America.*"

The Constitution became effective on June 21, 1788 when New Hampshire finally ratified it.

Virginia finally ratified the Bill of Rights on December 15, 1791.

That history brought me to the Tippecanoe County Courthouse to exercise my rights as a citizen and juror in this great country. I am "We The People."

Examples of a tried and true government surrounded me in the courthouse and it waited for my fundamental principles and natural human nature to ratify history. It waited for me to write my own version of truth.

I descended the two flights of courthouse steps that just two days previously I had naively climbed, not knowing what was about to happen if chosen to serve on the jury. I had no idea that the whole process would change me, change my attitude, and change my heart. I was proud of myself and the judicial system.

I walked past the four statues depicting influential people in Tippecanoe County, past the paintings hanging on the walls and past the two huge wall murals illustrating Indiana history. I walked past the antique black, metal elevator that I never used, but kept wanting to ride. I walked past the ornate oak trimmed decorative oak doors and past signs that informed people of different governmental functions that took place in the courthouse. I walked past people yet waiting to do their business in the courthouse, whether it be government business or court business. I sensed a few people were waiting for their trial, for their judgment, for their possible future alteration. I walked out of the courthouse a more educated man for having spent two days as a juror in Superior Court One.

I arrived home to first see my American flag welcoming and reminding me of what an amazing country in which I lived. I was in the Navy fifty years ago. I loved my country and the flag then and love it even more today. I gained a little more love for both country and flag during the past couple of days doing jury duty.

# Knowing Best

Tyrannical ideas
never die, but
arrogantly rise
when a despot
feigns to know
better than many.

One superior,
arrogant
acting person
can espouse
biases like a
hovering hawk.

A tyrant
often deems
to know
social order
and control
by arrogance.

Freedom thrives
when naturally
enlightened
eagles soar
higher than a
despotic hawk.

# Imperfect Birds

Cold wind
provokes
thoughts of
flying while
time waiting.
Defensive fall
colors are
valiantly
disappearing
too soon.

Coerced
birds ignore
present air,
wishing warm
breezes for
better flying.
Winter's norm
settles-in with
purifying snow,
alarming vulnerable
green things.
A natural world
teaches rest and
seasonal joy, and
inconvenient
cold wind
causes it
to be perfect.

Tolerant
birds accept
natural change
intuitively and
fly south,

but most stay,
fight elements,
seek liberty,
die trying or
live free.

Returning
spring is
wonderful.
It takes
time and
patience to
recover from
winter.
A principled
calendar
doesn't lie, and
reveals that
freedom
is for
perfect
seasons and
imperfect
birds.

# Like Platelets

How did our
Republic get tattered
so unnoticeably and
freedom get stained
so deceptively?

One man's ideas
sounded good while
he sought victory
like seldom before.
America accepted
his shifting policies
like earthen plates,
silently fracturing
government itself.
And, in crevices
profound, a splitting
philosophy appeared,
allowing government
expansion to be
disguised as progress.
Our national spirit
aged, got reformed and
progressed.

How did our
Republic get tattered
so unnoticeably and
freedom get stained
so deceptively?

# Fractural Spirit

Freedom roamed
for a while with
grace and ease,
then legally and
morally found
people guilty of
complacency.

Without knowing
legitimate self,
America accepted
different truths and
hidden agendas.
Epic initiatives
altered authority and
social contracts.
Freedom soared
above unscathed
mountains briefly.
Then slowly
it unwillingly
declined as
choice wilted and
rightful equality
deteriorated.

Freedom roamed
for a while with
grace and ease,
then legally and
morally found
people guilty of
complacency.

# Wheat Field Blowing

Unlike straw
floating in
wheat field wind,
unalienable rights
don't rush carelessly
across a nation's
defining history.
Harvested
memories
will not scatter
like wheat straw,
but remain
like precious
thrashed grain.
No man can or
should redefine
God given rights.
Oh, some seek
self-reward,
pretending
good for all,
but they
advocate same
failed ideas,
like straw upon
wheat fields
blowing.

# Picture Album

Old wistful
album
pictures of
past statesmen
lay lifeless.
Faded letters
seek assurance
of existence.

People wonder
no more
while learning
history as
it becomes
relevant again
in new hearts,
minds, souls.

Freedom seems
lazy at times,
yet it will not
depart easily
once brilliantly
exposed and
definably given
to new citizens.

# Roosevelt

My name is,
Roosevelt, and
I hustle
fulfillment,
making
tomorrow
seem like
yesterday
with much
learned.
In my mind,
ideas flow like
creeks and
rivers waiting
command.
I construct
self-esteem
with those
flowing
creeks and
rivers.
I oblige
few while
pretending
conditions and
government
controls for
many.
My name is
Roosevelt, and
I hustle
fulfillment.

# Contrast

Our country was
like a well behaved
child doing small
wrongs things, and
then an unusual man
misguided conduct,
broke hearts and
made many desire
rectification.
Like a child doing
small wrongs,
our nation soon did
not recognize
wrongdoing.
Lack of contrast amid
good and bad,
right and wrong,
made our flag wilt,
government falter
and liberty fade.
Small cuts became
serious wounds and
our country staggered.
We walked casually
while rain washed
minds as torrential
storms thrived.
We, however,
weathered chaos and
like unruly children
doing better things,
we sought renewed
freedom.

# Someone

I might be crazy,
in this mind state or
I might be onto
something special.
I'm probably fooling
myself in believing
I deserve special
treatment as
might working
callused hands
deserve lotion.
I wish not to
change my ways,
for in that gesture,
I might hear
reality lecture
truthful words.
I care not to
hear truth or
at least not just
right now for in
fragile mind state,
security is dissolving
while confidence
is disintegrating.
Times are tough,
future is bleak and
abuse is seeking
my obtuse attention.
I hope someone
comes along to save
thickheaded me.

# Passive Swing

We have all sat
on an outdoor swing
one time or another,
storm sensing,
thunder listening and
lightening seeing.
What makes us
run for shelter,
realize danger and
alter our location?
Yes, we have
sense enough to
get indoors and
out of destructive
tempest doom as
aggressive storms
threaten our
pensive existence.
Someone is calling
for new rights.
A new rights list
is accumulating.
We take notice of
near thundering
change and
far lightening
catastrophe.
Oh, we've been
here before
sitting in a
passive swing,
listening, sensing,
ignoring.

# Divinity

Oh, amazing
human nature
take my hand,
lead me onward
towards freedom
from a ship's
porthole view.
Lead me in
revived zest for
your hand is
my hand,
your way is
my way,
your freedom is
my freedom.
Sacred rights
emulate
your grace as
my future
necessitates
your help.
Allow my
nature to be
heavenly host
supported for
I need
Divinity as
I prepare to
disembark
my ship and
encounter a
new world.

# I Squint to See

My college campus
has three buildings
standing on solid
constitutional ground.
Representative
humanity flows
in and out of them
like rivers seeking
to serve and present
law and order.
Each building has
own function and is
separated by eclectic
power needs.
Feet trample
grass between
tread intended
sidewalks while
moving in disorder.
I squint to see
tomorrow's
humanity replacing
today's mortality
on a never ending
governmental
merry-go-round.
Higher learning
planners sought a
more perfect college
for new minds
to cultivate a
philosophy of
statesmen art.

# Wind

Intellectual ropes
intertwine and
tangle minds.
Power expansion is
parting people,
firmly seeking and
regulating control.

Men speaks of a
Great Society,
spewing old
worn messages,
some painfully
over reaching,
pitifully seeking.

Leaders ineptly
flounder in
liberty and
freedom speak,
using turbulent
times to rip and
tear at fragile
national fabric.

Caught between
yes and no, and
objective and
subjective,
citizens get
confused by
altruistic beliefs.

# Tending Silt

Resourceful seeds
planted at dawn,
enter earthy loam by
settler's hands with
apt knowledge and
felt compassion.

Humanity of
their inner soul is
like rain on seeds,
germinating
buried grace from
God's unique hand.

A community of
planters from seeds
grow stalks into
blooms that become
fruit for food and
again spiritual seeds.

So resources of
man and nature
bear bounty by
seeding Republic
evolution while
tending freedom.

But, corn and
wheat alone don't
make angels smile,
for it's God's
nature that makes
everything grow.

# Scattered Seed

Liberated creatures
embraced ideas, and
in graceful time came
enlightenment and
intellectual embrace.
Weightless ideas created
natural stepping-stones
that caused an enchanted
path to freedom's
understanding way.

Like strewn rudiments,
liberty seeds helplessly
waited to germinate
luscious pasture seeds,
willing to dream by
accepting selfless rain.
Forefathers breached
rational barriers, and
found revelation and
inevitable revolution.

People moaned and
groaned from accepting
events and yet embraced
emerging answers while
heroes fostered courage.
One man was outwardly,
inwardly and gracefully
lifted high enough to
write a Declaration
Of Independence.

# Reaganwood

A chain saw cuts
inner hardwood
of a tree felled
from pressures
beyond its control.
Engine roars,
smoke drifts,
chips fly while a
wood carver seeks a
perfect wood piece
from which to
turn a nearly
perfect bowl.

How many times has
he sawed such wood?
How many times has
he turned a perfect
piece of timber?

Chain saw stays
its destruction,
cutting pieces of
nature's essence.
Wood carver then
cuts smaller pieces
that helplessly fall
waiting judgment
and assessment.
Sawing achieves
ideal wood pieces
for his dexterous
lathe turning hands.

His saw rests,
no longer needed.
He rolls pieces
by looking eyes
for possibilities.
Hundred percent
perfection is
impossible.
Eighty percent
is better than a
lesser percent
whether bowl,
law or union.

He carries selected
pieces from a
silent forest where
wood chips and
log parts lay
waiting another
wood carver's eye.
A forest always
waits natural or
manmade disasters
without a plan or
definition of
conservative care.

How many times has
he sawed such wood?
How many times has
he turned a perfect
piece of timber?

# Tasting Life

In a conscious place
where secrets lie,
truth ferments like
intoxicating wine
that makes a covert
man feel vulnerable.

Life feeds soul,
mind cultivates
cause and effect
ideas that create
individual results of
spiritual essence.

Accrued wisdom
ferments truth
through time and
space that too soon
place one's faith
where angels gather.

# Freedom Rejoices

In clever core
lies one's soul
that senses and
gathers, and
remembers
freedom
that infused
mind while
experiencing a
magnificent
journey.

Each caring
individual
is like a
pearl,
created by an
oyster's
sand grain
of soul,
left free to
naturally
flourish.

# Self-governing

I wish to conceal
my weaknesses,
but continue to
govern myself by
speaking softly and
carrying a big stick.

I wish to veil
my faults from
faith thieves and
freedom hoodlums
impending poise
without penalty.

I wish to briefly
hunker down,
sit it out and hone
several ticks, and
learn to speak an
aggressive language.

No one knows me,
for in my soul
lives a freedom
fighter with covert
strengths and
brawling skills.

# You

You are
one who
suffered a
scalding
kettle,
believing
it soothing
broth at
Valley Forge.
You are
one who
caught
bullets,
thinking them
love notes at
Concord.
You are
one who gave
courageous
orders,
thinking
they
would save
freedom at
Trenton.

# Train to Philadelphia

You learned
greatness on
roads and
battlefields.
Weight
toting made
your mind
reap grand
thoughts.
You silently
remained
humble
like an
exploited grape
becoming
fine wine.
You were
reluctant
to drink of
yourself,
get liberally
drunk and
catch a train to
Philadelphia.
You urged
ominous
Founders to
think and
write a
Constitution.
You made
eyes see,
ears hear and
leaders follow.

# Liberty Writing

People heard freedom,
tasted its sweetness and
felt its imagined reality.
A trusting cradle exposed
infant laws and child like
controls of invalid charm.
A baby nation lay awake,
waiting a hand to sway as
spiritual entities activated
its vibrant, colonial mind.

A nation reached like a
perfect storm front with
valid castle destruction.
An old nation faltered,
new one arose while
men in ballet slippers and
white wigs flinched.
Long shadows warned,
strength and conviction
served eviction paper.

Fervent energy spoke,
supremacy listened while
many defeats haunted, but
victories implied triumph.
People fretted no more
for a few freedom steps,
like a gold piece dropping,
documents shared and
colonists walked liberty
across a continent.

# I Reflect

I embrace life
again today,
physically and
mentally pursuing
time, space and
insight extension.
I fight and
mindfully attack
apathy and failure.
It's a bitter
pill to swallow.

I reach
my zenith in
spite of wavering
highs, mediums and
lows.
Bell curved life
forms rugged
visages to an
old man's
furrowed face.
Each wrinkle
writes history.

I yet smile,
reflect wisdom,
cast a shadow while
humbly reflecting
time, space and
aware material.
Ignorance yet
teases me with
potent sweetness.
I taste it with

reckless appetite
like chocolate
ice cream or
apple pie.

But, I realize
I cannot fight
ignorance,
apathy and failure.
I have little
choice other
than to embrace
life through
time, space and
courage.

For now,
I continue to
taste chocolate with
reckless abandon
like a little boy
not knowing
ignorant appeal of
apathy, sorrow,
failure.
I finally find
passing is not
such a bitter
pill to swallow.

# *Conclusion*

It all started about two thousand years ago with Socrates, Aristotle and Plato. It took about three hundred years to build a nation. It took three years to build the courthouse in which I served jury duty. It took two days to determine that we could not determine guilt or innocence of a man being tried for soliciting sex from a minor and soliciting pornography. I think it will take years for me to not be impressed by serving on a jury.

I have written my sketchy recollection of what took place during jury duty and the effect it had on me. I have included many poems about our form of government and the process of gaining, maintaining and protecting freedom. Freedom is the beginning of the natural human living experience and without liberty there can be no continuum of the great American experiment.

Even though we could not agree on whether the defendant was guilty or innocent, we did give him a reprieve from a bad conclusion. Let us remember that he was innocent until proven guilty; for now he is yet innocent. I don't believe that he will be tried again because the prosecution didn't have enough evidence. They apparently had a good lawyer representing the state because soon after the trial he was asked to serve as a federal prosecutor. That surely meant the prosecution in this trial had a good advocate.

I walked back to my Jeep parked on the jury parking lot with my cohort in justice, First Lady, we talked about speaking with the defense lawyer before heading to the parking lot. He further solidified our feelings about holding out for an innocent conclusion. We failed to get our way for the defendant, but I think we did the next best thing. We did not let him get convicted of a crime we both believed he didn't commit. We shook hands and looked each other in the eyes and non-verbally said "job well done." I yet do not know her name and will probably never see her again. I think we made a bond that only lasted two days, but the memory of that bonding will last the rest of my life.

I know most people think it's not a big thing doing jury duty, except for high profile trials, and I probably thought similarly a short time ago. I now see what we did in the courtroom and the deliberation room was a big thing, an important thing, a constitutional thing and a freedom thing.

Serving justice is a mighty big deal. It's a reformation of our form of government. It's a tribute to the Founders of this country. It's a protective action to life, liberty and the pursuit of happiness.

# *About the Author*

Phillip has long been a poet, maturing into a thoughtful poetic man who has always sought learning about himself and his environment. He's a person who has sought justice, whether on the playground at six years of age on the basketball court at sixteen, in the military at age twenty-two, in the classroom at forty-five or in the courtroom at age seventy-three.

Phillip attempts to express his feelings, emotions and thoughts with limited words in a concise format that causes one to think about certain situations and subjects. He has taken a path of helping others "Know Thyself" also all his life. He is a natural teacher and cannot change that fact no matter what situation he finds himself. He has taught own children, students and employees. He has more importantly, taught himself. One could say he is trying to educate the general public in own modest, limited way while yet learning.

His history and experience has to some degree matured into wisdom. He began life naked and crying, but wishes to end life fully clothed and smiling. He is like most everyone, not afraid of dying, but just doesn't want it to hurt. He wants the return trip to heaven to be a smooth and graceful experience. He says, "I just want a few days to say good-bye and have a good enough mind to experience the once in a lifetime event. I hope it's not too much to ask."

Phillip has a certain optimism in his writing while recognizing the pain and suffering of humanity. I think he can literally hear human nature moan, groan and whimper. I also think he can feel human nature cheer, exult and celebrate. His says, "I desire to draw cautious pictures at dawn, vigilant pictures at noon and realized pictures at dusk; then paint and convert thoughtful conclusions that even a blind person can see."

Phillip hopes you will show mercy towards him for his attempt to be intellectual and spiritual with limited ability and skill. He tries to convert what's in his mind to paper while sharing feelings without revealing emotions, yet relents mental and physical privacy for the sake of revealing soul. He wants to return to heaven with what he calls his "soul suitcase" full of earthly experiences and then hear God say, "Well done."

He has high hope for self-territory expansion through writing, but low public acceptance hope for his philosophy. His only defense for being what he is and doing what he does is to forever learn to "Know Thyself."

Printed in the United States
By Bookmasters